Adaptive Counseling and Therapy

George S. Howard
Don W. Nance
Pennie Myers

■ ■ ■ ■ ■ ■ ■ ■ ■ ■ ■ ■ ■ ■

Adaptive Counseling
and Therapy

A Systematic Approach to Selecting
Effective Treatments

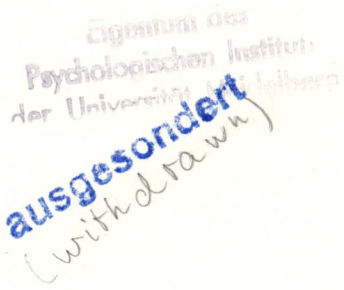

Jossey-Bass Publishers

San Francisco • London • 1987

ADAPTIVE COUNSELING AND THERAPY
A Systematic Approach to Selecting Effective Treatments
by George S. Howard, Don W. Nance, and Pennie Myers

Copyright © 1987 by: Jossey-Bass Inc., Publishers
433 California Street
San Francisco, California 94104
&
Jossey-Bass Limited
28 Banner Street
London EC1Y 8QE

Library of Congress Cataloging-in-Publication Data

Howard, George S.
  Adaptive counseling and therapy.

  (The Jossey-Bass social and behavioral science series)
  Bibliography: p. 205
  Includes index.
  1. Psychotherapy. 2. Counseling. 3. Psychiatry—Differential therapeutics. I. Nance, Don. II. Myers, Pennie. III. Title. IV. Series. [DNLM: 1. Counseling—methods. 2. Psychotherapy—methods. WM 420 H849a]
  RC480.5.H69   1987   616.89'14   86-33756
  ISBN 1-55542-038-9 (alk. paper)

Manufactured in the United States of America

The paper in this book meets the guidelines for permanence and durability of the Committee on Production Guidelines for Book Longevity of the Council on Library Resources.

JACKET DESIGN BY WILLI BAUM

FIRST EDITION

Code 8714

The Jossey-Bass
Social and Behavioral Science Series

Contents

10. Adaptive Counseling and Therapy:
     Summary and Future Directions   200

     References   205

     Index   211

Preface

Our purpose in writing *Adaptive Counseling and Therapy: A Systematic Approach to Selecting Effective Treatments* is to present a model within which other theories of psychotherapy can be organized and understood. We hope and believe that the presentation of a pragmatic integrative model will clarify and improve clinical practice. Models and theories related to the practice of counseling and psychotherapy are ever expanding. More and more practitioners consider themselves eclectic psychotherapists. Confusion and uncertainty concerning what treatment approaches to use with which clients are natural by-products of the proliferation of psychotherapeutic theories and models. In addition, an unhealthy competition exists among the proponents of various psychotherapeutic schools of thought. Adaptive Counseling and Therapy (ACT) provides a conceptual framework that diminishes the confusion created by the smorgasbord of psychotherapeutic choices and provides the eclectic practitioner with a systematic method for selecting the most effective treatment for each particular client. The ACT model is also an antidote to ''my theory is better than your theory'' thinking; as such, we hope it will encourage more collaboration in approaches to complex mental health problems.

Who Should Read This Book?

This is a book for clinical practitioners in fields such as psychology, counseling, psychiatry, social work, family therapy,

pastoral counseling, and medicine who daily undertake the task
of providing a variety of mental health services. We believe that
the concepts presented here will be useful to practitioners no
matter what set of letters follow their names or what organizations provide their primary professional associations. The model
is especially pertinent for the eclectic practitioner who can benefit
from a framework within which to arrange diverse theoretical
approaches and a model that will help in selecting effective treatment plans. Practitioners who find themselves ''stuck'' with a
particular client or with a particular type of client will find that
ACT can help them analyze the problem and redirect the therapy
process. ACT can also assist clinicians when they are called on
to explain their treatment choice (charting, case review, insurance filing, legal questions, and so forth). In such cases, ACT
not only helps in the selection of an effective treatment approach
but provides a tool for communicating the rationale behind that
selection. In addition, practitioners involved in the training and
supervision of other professionals will appreciate the ACT model
as a training aid. Supervisors can use ACT to help those with
whom they work to select the most effective treatment for clients
and to understand why certain treatment approaches are effective while others are not.

We also hope this book will be embraced by students in
professional preparation programs and by the professionals who
teach and train them. Reactions of colleagues who read various
drafts of the book during its development have been very positive
about the usefulness of the model as an integrative framework
for the various courses in the professional preparation process.
We believe the book has potential as a text for courses and seminars focused on the practice of counseling and psychotherapy.

Colleagues with research interests and skills may glean
heuristic value from this book. We believe the model has great
potential for integrating existing research and for serving as a
framework for developing productive lines of empirical inquiry.

Background on the ACT Model

ACT as an organizing system for therapy has had a long
gestation period. Its history began when Don W. Nance and

Pennie Myers first learned about situational leadership and recognized that the basic constructs of situational leadership applied to the practice of therapy as well as to the management of business. When Nance, as director of the Counseling Center at Wichita State University, introduced his staff to his beginning formulation of ACT, the model was greeted with enthusiasm. Those therapists found ACT an excellent tool, not only for understanding what they were already doing in therapy but also, and more importantly, for treatment planning and redirecting treatment that was not working effectively. For the next few years, the model was presented to various groups of helping professionals, always with the same positive response. At that point, we realized that some parallel research work would strengthen ACT. George S. Howard and his students at the University of Notre Dame worked diligently at this task. Ten years of work with ACT resulted in our writing a monograph to introduce ACT to our professional colleagues. That monograph and the responses of five readers appear in *The Counseling Psychologist* (Howard, Nance, and Myers, 1986). Although both the monograph and this book describe ACT, they are quite different from one another. This book presents the model specifically for practitioners and for those who train and supervise them. It relies heavily on case material to enrich the reader's understanding of ACT and to help readers apply ACT concepts to their clinical practice.

   While our intention at this time is simply to introduce the basic principles of the ACT model and demonstrate their applicability to clinical practice, we firmly believe in the ability of this model to deal with a variety of specialized therapeutic situations. For example, marital and family therapy, group therapy, and counseling with minority populations and with those from other cultural backgrounds are all potential applications. In addition, we believe that the model can be applied with excellent results to supervision with students and colleagues. Since these topics are not the subject of this book, they remain to be addressed by ourselves and by others who are interested in adding to the understanding of the relationship between ACT and clinical practice.

Overview of the Contents

The first chapter of *Adaptive Counseling and Therapy* under-scores the need for an integrative model, presents brief descrip-tions of existing integrative models, and acknowledges the model's roots. The reader is invited to complete an inventory concerning his or her style as a therapist as a learning tool for understanding and applying the ACT model. The model is introduced in Chapter Two. In Chapter Three major approaches to psychotherapy are compared to ACT in order to illustrate the integrative nature of this model. The behaviors and char-acteristics of therapists are the subject of Chapter Four, and the Therapist Style Inventory presented in the first chapter is discussed. Chapter Five focuses on client characteristics as they pertain to the selection of appropriate treatment approaches and therapist behaviors. Illustrative case material is presented in Chapters Six and Eight, while Chapter Seven addresses the specific issues involved in assessing clients and planning treat-ment according to the ACT model. Chapter Nine uses the ACT model to analyze a number of cases described in the literature. In addition to summarizing the main points of ACT, Chapter Ten looks at clinical uses of ACT and its specific value as a tool for the eclectic practitioner. Throughout the book clinical ex-amples are provided that will help readers translate a concep-tual model into an applied clinical tool.

The preface comes first in the book but last in its writing. Since we are writing to practitioners who frequently share our interest in the process as well as the product, we think it is ap-propriate to share some process information, especially since our process in writing this book fits the ACT model. A wide range of tasks are involved in conceptualizing and writing any book. Authors bring a variety of competencies, motives, and confidence levels to such tasks. This book required three co-authors to combine their talents and energies in a truly collab-orative process. Don W. Nance conceptualized the application of situational leadership to psychotherapy, envisioned the inte-grative capacity of the concepts, and provided the initial transla-tion of the model by applying it in his own professional practice of psychotherapy and supervision. George S. Howard brought research and writing skills and boundless confidence to the process. His "can do" attitude is infectious. His notable record of publication and stature in the field lent credibility and respect to a fledgling model. In addition, he directed the initial research efforts. Pennie Myers brought to this endeavor her excellent organizational skills, her ability to see the important points to be made, the skill to present those points using a clear, cogent writing style, and a wealth of clinical experience. She could understand reviewers' comments and see which changes needed to be made and how to make them. The cases presented were drawn frequently from her personal clinical and supervisory experience. Her background in marital and family therapy enriched the range of clinical applications. With energy from all and with the necessary direction of and support for each other, the task was accomplished.

February 1987

George S. Howard
Notre Dame, Indiana

Don W. Nance
Wichita, Kansas

Pennie Myers
Wichita, Kansas

The Authors

George S. Howard is chairperson and associate professor of the Department of Psychology, University of Notre Dame. He has a B.A. degree (1970) in psychology from Marist College and M.A. (1972) and Ph.D. (1975) degrees in counseling psychology from Southern Illinois University. Howard has concentrated on theoretical, methodological, and philosophical problems in such applied areas of psychology as counseling, clinical, educational, and organizational psychology. He is a fellow of the American Psychological Association and has published more than seventy-five articles in refereed psychological journals. He is also the author of *Basic Research Methods in the Social Sciences* (1985) and *Dare We Develop a Human Science?* (1986).

Don W. Nance is director of counseling and associate professor at Wichita State University. Under his direction, the Counseling Center there has more than tripled in size and become an internship training site approved by the American Psychological Association and affiliated with the Wichita Collaborative Psychology Internship Program. He developed one of the first fee-for-service counseling center programs in the country. Throughout his professional career, he has remained a practicing psychotherapist. Consultation and training with businesses, health care organizations, and governmental and educational institutions is his other major professional focus. In addition to journal articles and monographs, he is coauthor, with Pennie Myers, of *The Upset Book: A Guide to Dealing with Upset*

xvii

Persons. He received his B.A. degree (1964) in psychology from the University of Redlands and his M.A. (1967) and Ph.D. (1968) degrees in counseling psychology from the University of Iowa.

Pennie Myers is marriage and family services director at Wichita State University. She serves on the gerontology faculty and teaches in the areas of counseling, families, and aging. She received her B.A. degree (1973) from Wichita State University in psychology and sociology, her M.A. degree (1975) in psychology from the same institution, and an Ed.D. degree (1983) in counseling from the International Graduate School. Along with her roles as a clinician and educator, Myers applies her systems orientation and clinical skills as a consultant to business, educational, and governmental organizations. She is an approved supervisor for the American Association for Marriage and Family Therapy and has supervised numerous training grants and contracts totaling several hundred thousand dollars. In addition to a number of journal articles (Myers was previously published under the name P. M. Cohen), Myers has coauthored *The Upset Book: A Guide to Dealing with Upset Persons* (with Don W. Nance, 1986).

Adaptive Counseling
and Therapy

1

▦ ▦ ▦ ▦ ▦ ▦ ▦ ▦ ▦ ▦ ▦ ▦ ▦

What Is
Adaptive Counseling
and Therapy (ACT)?

It is a rare occurrence for those of us who practice the art and science of psychotherapy to find ourselves with a case so dramatic that it attracts the attention of large segments of the professional community. More often, despite the poignancy and individuality of each client's story, the people we see in our offices represent fairly predictable categories of human behavior and experience. The ideas presented in this book are rooted in many years of clinical practice with a rather ordinary and only occasionally dramatic caseload. The pragmatic value of these developing ideas was nourished by clinical observation and application. Eventually, our hypotheses were subjected to the scrutiny of research.

This introduction to adaptive counseling and therapy is aimed at making everyday psychotherapy easier for those of us who are professionally engaged in its practice and at providing a greater likelihood of success for those who use counseling and psychotherapeutic services. Adaptive counseling and therapy (ACT) is intended to be useful in case conceptualization and in the application of effective treatment planning. With these objectives in mind, we begin by introducing you to James, a thirty-six-year-old client who was seen in therapy by a colleague some years ago. During the initial three sessions of therapy, James recounted a history that, for the most part, included failure in every aspect of his life. Unable to maintain a job and unable to complete a ten-year flirtation with graduate school, James's adult life had been peppered with odd jobs and intermittent attempts to complete an advanced degree in anthropology. James was seeking counseling at the request of his wife, who was threatening to leave him if he did not "shape up." For the last fifteen years, James's wife had been the emotional and financial mainstay of the family, which also included two teenage children. Other tidbits of information gathered early by the therapist included years of promiscuous sex, long-term drug abuse, and an incredible ability for taking advantage of most of the people in his life. The only motivation for change appeared to be James's fear of losing his wife or, perhaps more accurately, the financial stability his wife provided. James's therapist was now faced with the thorny task of developing a treatment plan—a plan that might change James's behavior.

James's therapist, like many counselors, was faced with a "cafeteria dilemma" when it came to selecting a therapeutic treatment plan and style: Which therapy should she use, and how much of this or that therapist behavior would help her client with his problem? There are so many therapeutic theories and techniques available today that selecting the most appropriate therapy is a difficult decision for even the most experienced clinician, let alone the novice or student. Where can a therapist look when trying to conceptualize the best avenue for change for a client? It is precisely this dilemma—the selection of the most appropriate treatment plan—that this book was written to address. The primary goal of adaptive counseling and therapy is to provide a way of organizing all the theories about how people change in order to make treatment planning a methodical process rather than a haphazard one. We will return to James and his therapist in some detail in Chapter Two.

Before we can address the issue of organizing therapy techniques to best serve our clients, it is necessary to understand why and how such a proliferation of ideas about therapy has developed. Perhaps the answer to this question lies in the complexity of human nature itself. Students of human behavior have been faced with a range of behavior for which no simple explanations are possible. Obviously, if there is no easy way to explain what makes people the way they are, then it follows that there can be no easy way to explain how to make people change through a therapeutic process. It is not surprising, then, that contemporary ideas about therapy are the result of a long intellectual search by theoreticians and practitioners. The creation of new therapeutic concepts, as well as disputing the relative merits and shortcomings of each perspective, has kept the helping profession busy for most of its history. When an existing theory has failed to explain human behavior adequately, either that theory has been expanded further or a splinter group of dissenters has broken away to develop another point of view. For the most part, this has not been a friendly process.

This expansion or splintering can be illustrated by looking at the history of Freudian and neo-Freudian thought, which is filled with theoretical and interpersonal strife. What began as a group of thinkers who shared a belief in Freud's psychodynamic explanation of human behavior eventually disintegrated because of incestuous family disputes within the inner circle. Adler, Jung, and Horney all departed from Freud, wishing to improve some perceived weakness in his theory. Freud's theoretical descendants did not present their refined psychodynamic explanations simply as welcome expansions or additions to the theory. These changes were offered, and therefore perceived, as attacks.

Traditionally, proponents of new theories have felt the need to debunk their predecessors and contemporaries rather than appreciating what another perspective might contribute. This can be seen throughout the psychotherapeutic literature. In B. F. Skinner's work, for example, one finds numerous disparaging comments on the psychodynamic school (Skinner, 1971). Similarly, Carl Rogers (1961) argued against a psychodynamic understanding and later against behavioral theory, seemingly to justify offering a humanistic theory.

Those in the helping professions are sometimes encouraged to adopt one of the major theoretical perspectives as their own and to apply that approach to the myriad problems with which they must cope. However, real-life practice often demon-

strates the inadequacies of graduate education or a particular
training program. For most of us, experience has shown that
a single way of understanding human behavior does not have
universal applicability to every psychological problem.

Just as one theoretical approach to therapy is generally
not successful with a range of behavior problems, so proponents
of this or that theoretical orientation can usually point to a particular problem as one with which their approach is especially
successful. The reason for this kind of "natural selection" is
discussed in detail in Chapter Three. What bears reiterating here
is that psychotherapy embraces a broad range of theory about
what makes people tick and what helps people to change. The
value of this breadth and richness in the field cannot be over-
estimated. The major thesis in our book is that different therapy
situations require different therapeutic interventions. Fortu-
nately, there are many therapies from which to choose. The key
to making the best selection for an intervention is to make the
selection in a systematic way by using a specific set of criteria.
Adaptive counseling and therapy offers a theoretical tool to
facilitate this process.

The Rise of Eclecticism

Psychotherapy has gone through several periods when a
pet theory was in special favor and large numbers of practitioners
were aligning themselves accordingly. At the present time, a
minority of therapists report strict theoretical allegiance. Indeed,
the preponderance of therapists identify with some form of eclecticism. One sign of this trend is the recent publication of the
first *Handbook of Eclectic Psychotherapy* (Norcross, 1986).

Garfield and Kurtz (1977) documented this trend by track-
ing a rather dramatic shift in the theoretical orientation of
psychologists. While their survey evidenced a decline in the
percentage of psychologists adhering to a psychoanalytic orientation (19 percent in 1977 as opposed to 41 percent in a 1974
survey), almost 55 percent of those surveyed identified themselves as eclectics. At the same time, other current orientations
such as learning theory and humanistic approaches were showing only slight gains in preference by therapists.

What does it mean to be an eclectic? Some theoretical purists might argue that being an eclectic is synonymous with being indecisive, wishy-washy, or confused. Eclectics have been characterized as fad-chasers, opportunists, and fence-sitters. Such attacks are typically offered by strong proponents of particular schools of thought who view theoretical purity as a *sine qua non* for therapists. Purists consider theoretical fidelity (even if it means being faithful to the "wrong" theory) as preferable to the promiscuity of eclecticism.

A more positive view sees eclecticism as an answer to the complexity and multidimensional nature of human problems. According to eclectics, interventions using multiple channels of influence stand the greatest likelihood of success. Clearly, our book is based on this positive view of an eclectic approach to therapy. We now offer a few brief case descriptions to illustrate the potential value of therapeutic eclecticism:

- Mary C. is a thirty-five-year-old, bright, articulate, recently divorced mother of two. Her therapeutic goals are to complete the grieving process related to her divorce and to find meaningful ways to restructure her life in her new role as a single woman. She appears to be highly motivated to accomplish these goals.
- Following his third drunk-driving arrest, Charlie M., a fifty-one-year-old salesman, is sentenced to appear for counseling. The court's goal is for Charlie to be cured of his drinking problem. Charlie's goal is to comply with the court so as not to lose his driver's license. He has little interest in stopping his drinking.
- Alan, a twenty-one-year-old recent college graduate, has just been released from the hospital following an acute psychotic episode. He describes a strong religious component to his current thinking. He is very anxious about his future career and relationship goals and is seriously contemplating joining a religious order. He wants help in therapy but is confused and unsure about what he needs.

It would not be unusual for a therapist to see a potpourri of cases like the ones described here on any given day. It seems

obvious that each of these cases may require a different therapeutic approach. On the surface, Mary appears to be well functioning and seeking adjustment to a difficult life situation. Charlie, on the other hand, seems to have a pattern of problematic
behavior. Both Alan and Mary are seeking help, whereas Charlie
is an unwilling participant. Diversity in people and diversity
in therapy explain why many therapists embrace some form of
eclecticism. To use existing theories about human behavior
through an eclectic approach seems more efficient than to continue searching for some theory of human behavior that would
explain and prescribe for every conceivable set of human possibilities.

The recurring problem with eclecticism has been the lack
of an organizing framework. Despite the frequent "seat of the
pants" selection of an appropriate therapy for a client, the eclectic helper is indeed in danger of doing little more than making
random therapeutic choices. The current body of therapeutic
knowledge needs to be systematized in order to help therapists
decide when they should use this or that therapeutic approach.
Predictions about the future of psychotherapy forecast that integrative theories will be the significant contributions in the years
to come. Allen Ivey (1980, p. 12) writes: "Finally, we may expect to find that new metatheoretical and integrative helping
theories will replace the competing models of the present. The
increasingly popular question, 'Which treatment for which individual (or system) at what time and under what conditions?'
will have some important beginning answers. Basic to any
metatheoretical statement that evolves will be an awareness of
person-environment transaction." Looking toward the year
2000, Leona Tyler, (1980, p. 134) claims: "By then the conflicts between theoretical systems, so prominent a feature of the
20th century scene, will have disappeared. Even now behavior-
ists are making a place for cognition within their framework,
humanists are concerning themselves with action as well as experience, and the main insights of psychoanalysis have been incorporated into personality theory."

But perhaps the most important evidence for eclecticism
comes from the extensive literature on the value of appropriate

treatment/client matching. (See, for example, Paul, 1967; Heller, Myers, and Kline, 1963; Parker, 1967.) ACT, our response to the need for a systematic organization of therapeutic techniques, specifically addresses the issue of appropriately matching the treatment to the client and the client's problems. While ACT is an integrative model that has the matching of treatment to client at its heart, it is certainly not the first attempt to integrate therapeutic theory.

Out of the proliferation of therapy approaches and the welter of studies of psychotherapy process, metatheoretical constructs have been emerging. This integrative trend has often been described in the psychological literature. (See, for example, Goldfried, 1980, 1982; Goldfried and Padower, 1982; Highlin and Hill, 1984; Ivey, 1980.) These integrative, metatheoretical models represent yet another way of structuring the thinking and practice of eclectic psychotherapists. Three systematic models that recommend various forms of therapeutic eclecticism are briefly reviewed here to situate our ACT approach within the broad context of an emerging eclecticism prevalent in psychotherapy today.

Lazarus's Multimodal Model. A survey of prevalent trends in counseling (Smith, 1982) reported that Lazarus's *Multimodal Behavior Therapy* (1976) was one of two works cited most frequently by professionals as representative of the present *Zeitgeist* in counseling and psychotherapy. Such an acknowledgment lends support to the suggestion that Lazarus's attempt at developing an integrative model (1971, 1976) offers an appropriate representative of this literature. Lazarus (1976) has defined his position as one of "technical eclecticism." He suggests that "to attempt a theoretical rapprochement is as futile as seriously trying to picture the edge of the universe. But to read through the vast mass of literature on psychotherapy in search of techniques can be clinically enriching and therapeutically rewarding" (1976, p. 321). The therapist is then thrust into the role of creative technician, using many techniques drawn from different sources. Adaptive counseling and therapy can also be considered an example of technical eclecticism in that the therapist uses ACT to select the best-matching therapeutic approach from the full range of possibilities "without also adhering to the theories or disciplines that spawned them" (Lazarus, 1976, p. 28). Both multimodal therapy and ACT are conceptual models that help make the selection of a treatment plan, including specific techniques, a systematic process.

Lazarus's model for providing systematic direction to the choice of technique centers upon seven principal aspects of client functioning that need to be assessed. According to Lazarus, a client's personality is organized around these seven modes of functioning and his systematic organization of therapeutic techniques focuses on influencing the client through each of these modalities. The seven categories—ongoing behavior, affective processes, sensations, images, cognitions, interpersonal relationships, and biological functions—are grouped under the acronym BASIC-ID. It is in terms of these seven modalities that the client's individual nuances and characteristics can be ascertained and used in selecting a multifaceted treatment strategy. ACT, by comparison, looks at different criteria in order to develop appropriate treatment choices. These criteria are discussed in detail in Chapter Two. Although ACT and multimodal therapy employ different criteria for assessing the client in terms of treatment planning, we believe that these two approaches are compatible if used in tandem. The eclectic clinician can apply Lazarus's modality profile to ascertain in what category or categories the client's problem is rooted—for example, is there a behavioral deficit or a problem with the client's thinking processes or both? Then the therapist can employ the criteria from ACT in order to determine specific therapist behaviors for conducting successful treatment. Moreover, various refinements and extensions of the 1976 multimodal model (Lazarus, 1981, 1985) complement ACT and provide the systematic eclectic therapist with innovative guidelines.

ACT does not attempt to look at the constructs of personality organization at all. ACT assumes that therapists already have a conceptual orientation related to how people develop and how change can occur. Therapists who call themselves eclectics are generally referring to an eclectic set of techniques in therapy. Most of us, presumably, have a foundation of understanding about people that supports our approach to helping people change. It would be more accurate to describe ACT as a model within which other models of psychotherapeutic change can be organized.

Beutler's Eclectic Psychotherapy Model. A second model that has attempted a synthesis of therapeutic techniques and counselor style has been postulated by Beutler (1983). His eclectic psychotherapy appears to represent an effort to respond to the previously mentioned body of literature suggesting common ingredients in psychotherapy. Beutler (1983, p. 2) contends that ''a theoretical system is needed that is sufficiently broad to encompass both the nonspecific and unique variables inherent in numerous theories, and yet specific enough to insure that these procedures can be applied in a reliable way.''

Beutler's theory, then, attempts to integrate perspectives derived from research and practice, yet the thrust of his ideas appears to move away from the application of specific techniques. Instead, Beutler focuses on adjusting styles and characteristics of therapists, as well as attending to a number of client variables. His model represents a systematic attempt to match therapist and client along three dimensions: personal compatibility, treatment technique (addressing the issue of choosing a treatment strategy for a specific population), and accommodations for client change (allowing the client's needs and goals to be flexible).

Beutler proposes that therapy is essentially a persuasion process in which the therapist attempts to influence the patient to undergo certain changes. Formal theory, then, is more of a backdrop for a set of assumptions and goals that are used in this interpersonal persuasion process. Underlying these ideas is the belief that psychotherapy is designed to confront an individual with evidence of dissonant elements in his or her belief system so that the person will evoke processes to resolve this dissonance. Consequently, the impact of technique in facilitating growth is minimized, while the therapist's interpersonal style (attractiveness, credibility, persuasive power, trustworthiness) assumes paramount importance. It is the perception of the client by the therapist that is of vital importance in determining the therapist's style.

The organization and administration of therapeutic strategies, then, revolves around a number of proposed treatment-determining and treatment-organizing variables. Initially, the goal of therapy is to build a strong therapeutic alliance in order to develop a compatibility that will evoke a sense of security in the client. Next, techniques and strategies are selected along three client variables: *symptom complexity* (assessed along a continuum from monosymptomatic, situation-specific habits to multisymptom neurotiform behavior patterns), *reactance potential* (a measure of the individual's resistance and investment in maintaining personal control and freedom), and *style of psychological defense* (internal and external styles of coping with internal and external conflict). An assessment of these variables leads to placing the client into a subcategory (for example, a highly reactant, externalizing individual exhibiting a monosymptomatic phobia). Specific counselor styles or treatment approaches are then associated with this client typology (for example, less controlling therapist employing a combination of experiential and cognitive therapies). There are two other treatment-organizing variables: the broad- or narrow-band focus of symptomology and four conflictual themes in which the client's problem may be framed (detachment, attachment, separation, and ambivalent patterns of dealing with the world).

Assessment assumes a place of prominence in Beutler's theory. Since psychotherapy is a process of encouraging value convergence, Beutler (1983) presents a number of guidelines for implementing a compatible matching of assumptive worlds of client and therapist. Essentially this process involves matching closely on sociodemographic variables while matching dissimilarly in terms of attachment needs and world threat. Psychotherapy for Beutler, then, becomes a process inducing cognitive dissonance. This process has a number of matching processes at its core and allows the flow of behavior between client and therapist to determine specific strategies and techniques.

Beutler's theory represents a heroic effort to synthesize the vast array of process studies examining therapist and client variables. It offers an attempt to systematically vary therapist style with a number of client characteristics. Clinically, his concepts such as reactance potential and style of defense are often difficult to measure and may evade the therapist's assessment attempts. Beutler slights technique organization and delineation, thus making directives to therapists less precise. Yet Beutler's "process eclecticism" does represent a worthwhile attempt to vary therapist style with client variables and seems worthy of future consideration.

ACT is predicated on a similar belief to Beutler's theory—a belief that the therapist's behavior should vary systematically with the client's variables. But, as mentioned earlier, ACT is not an attempt to organize therapy around a particular set of personality constructs. Rather, ACT gives a therapist a set of criteria for decisions related to treatment planning that can be used from the therapist's own conceptualization about human behavior. These criteria, described in the next chapter, are very much rooted in the here and now. The therapist does not have to dig deeply into the client's psyche to assess his or her functioning related to these criteria. They are a tool for deciding what form of treatment will best serve the client and what therapist style is likely to be most successful.

Brammer and Shostrom's Actualizing Counseling and Psychotherapy. Brammer and Shostrom's (1977) actualizing counseling and psychotherapy is a metatheoretical approach that draws more heavily on former theories than does either Beutler's or Lazarus's approach. The authors acknowledge their intellectual heritage in the following way:

Major conceptual contributions to actualizing counseling flow from Gestalt psychology, an aspect of the phenomenological view. Perls' ideas about perception, awareness, and encounter in the present moment are examples. The humanistic con-

tributions of Maslow on self-actualization, May on
human encounter, Rogers on sensitivity to feelings,
and Jourard on transparency and self-disclosure are
central also. Behavioral views such as those of
Krumboltz, Lazarus, and Bandura emphasize behavior reinforcement and specificity of client goals.
These views are important to actualizing counseling because they focus on problem-solving and actualizing goals desired by clients. Analytic views
have made their impact in the form of levels of functioning, with special focus on the ego, and the
phenomenon of defense [Brammer and Shostrom,
1977, pp. 70–71].

Out of this mix of diverse theoretical influences Brammer and Shostrom have crystallized a developmental view of
humans in which an individual achieves progressive awareness
and growth toward becoming an actualized person. This developmental perspective sees people growing through the following stages: the dependency stage (birth to two years), the independence stage (two to three years), the role-taking stage (four
to six years), the conformity stage (six to ten years), the transition stage (ten to thirteen years), the synthesis stage (thirteen
to twenty years), the experimentation stage (twenty to thirty-
five years), the consolidation stage (thirty-five to fifty years),
the involutional stage (forty-five to sixty years), and the evaluation stage (sixty years to the end of life).

The task of every individual is to grow through each of
these periods of development. Brammer and Shostrom are keenly
aware that a person is the product of all the experiences he or she
has had until the time he or she comes for counseling. Early for-
mative experiences are thought to exert important influences
on the type of adjustments made at later developmental levels.
But problems are a common denominator of growing, and it
is the succession of successful problem solutions that equips people with the resources to continue their psychological development. When problems become too difficult or too threatening
to resolve, one's developmental progress is arrested or one

develops a shield of defensive mechanisms that distorts and inhibits one's actualizing potentials.

Apart from this developmental focus, actualizing counseling also highlights the client's contemporary perceptual perspective (his or her unique outlook on life at that point in time). Additionally, there is an action or behavioral focus in actualizing counseling that keeps the therapist targeted upon real, behavioral problems (and concrete steps toward solutions) that the client is experiencing.

Actualizing counseling represents a complex and multifaceted system. In addition to the considerations mentioned above, Brammer and Shostrom (1977, p. 72) note:

> We see five dimensions comprising the actualizing point of view. A *philosophical* dimension is an essential consideration because of the emphasis on goals of actualization. We have a model of the kind of person who evolves in this growth process. This model incorporates a series of value judgments about the human condition and the nature of reality. The *structural* dimension, a schematic conceptualization of personality organization, is a kind of a cognitive map for viewing the actualizing process in a given moment of time. Closely related is the *dynamic* dimension, which emphasizes basic processes of growth and motivation. A *developmental* dimension includes much of what we know about human development. Finally, a *research* dimension is essential.

A great deal of material is subsumed under each of these five dimensions. The ability of actualizing counseling to handle the complexity and subtlety of human behavior and the therapeutic relationship may have been purchased at the cost of simplicity and ease in understanding.

ACT, similar to actualizing counseling, is a model that rests on the foundations of other psychological theory. ACT employs, as does actualizing counseling, a developmental perspective about human behavior. Not only is the client assessed developmentally in ACT, but the entire therapy process is viewed as developmental. ACT differs from actualizing counseling and psychotherapy because of ACT's total focus on specific criteria for selecting therapeutic interventions and because of ACT's dependence on the therapist's competence to conceptualize human behavior from his or her own perspective. Actualizing counseling and psychotherapy derives, as its title implies, from the humanistic tradition. ACT, in contrast, emanates from no single school of psychotherapy.

We do not mean to suggest that the three eclectic systems reviewed here are the only or the best integrative theoretical frameworks. Others have systematized their own metatheoretical perspectives. (See, for example, Prochaska, 1979; Garfield, 1980.) In fact, Brammer and Shostrom (1977) call for each therapist to consider developing what the authors refer to as his or her own creative synthesis or a unique theory or theories of psychotherapy. ACT is predicated on a belief that, at some level, most therapists have already done so.

ACT: Situational Leadership Applied to Therapy

ACT derives from a well-developed and well-respected model in the field of organizational behavior: behavioral leadership theory (Hersey and Blanchard, 1977). We were extremely impressed by the value of situational leadership in organizational settings. Recognizing the theory's utility in helping managers to select appropriate leadership styles for individual workers, it became clear that the theory had parallels in helping therapists to select appropriate therapy styles for individual clients. We acknowledge our debt to Hersey and Blanchard for developing a model that has such potential utility in the field of psychotherapy.

Hersey and Blanchard say that to be effective, managers need to use a broad range of leadership techniques. Management style is determined by the situation, including the worker's motivational level and skill. Just as managers should modify their behavior to match situational and worker needs, so we are asserting that therapists should modify their behavior to match situational and client needs. While managers can apply situational leadership theory in selecting an optimal style of managing, so too can therapists determine the appropriate therapy style through the application of ACT. Although the roles of therapist and leader are not entirely analogous, there are noteworthy similarities between the two. Because the role of the therapist in a counseling situation is surprisingly similar to the role of a leader in a business organization, the application of a situational leadership model to psychotherapy is a natural one.

The Therapist as Leader

A basic assumption in ACT is that, while different, the therapist's role and the leader's role have significant similarities. Asserting the similarity of the therapist's role in a counseling setting and the manager's role in an organizational context may be conceptually jarring. Clearly the contexts of therapist and manager are different. Moreover, the content on which a manager and a therapist focus their leadership efforts may be very different. Often the goals of a manager are different from those of a therapist. Such would be the case if a manager encouraged the passivity of a subordinate for exploitation reasons—clearly taboo (though, alas, not nonexistent) behavior for a therapist. The similarity between managers and therapists is based more upon similarities in the process of leadership and the process of therapy than on the content or context of their work. At least six key elements in the process link managers and therapists.

First, both therapist and manager are dependent on others for task accomplishments. The classic definition of management is "the accomplishment of organizational goals through the effort of other people." If you do the work yourself, you are not managing. Therapy is also, of necessity, working through or with other people to create, produce, or enable the accomplishment of certain therapeutic goals. It is quite clear that the therapist cannot accomplish the therapeutic tasks for the client. One of us remembers with frustration and embarrassment our first client. The client, whom we will call Harry, was a clinical psychologist (psychologists are frequently the most difficult clients) who reported having already seen thirteen different therapists. After a year of struggle, Harry's therapist finally realized that the only person in the therapy hour who was really working was the therapist. This fact became all too clear when Harry balked at having to pay the small fee for therapy not covered by his insurance. If the manager does all the work, he or she is not managing; if the therapist does all the work, he or she is not providing therapy. Therapy is a process that, when successful, enables clients to accomplish their goals.

Second, both therapist and manager wish to identify, mobilize, utilize, and enhance the motivation and abilities of the person to perform certain tasks. Good therapy, like good management, capitalizes on the qualities already existent in the client or worker and may try to build additional strengths and skills. If the client's or worker's resources are not immediately apparent, the therapist or the manager each may try to develop or add to the person's resources. Both the therapist and the manager work for the successful accomplishment of the appropriate tasks and goals.

Management may be more limited than therapy in the type of task required. An assembly line worker may be hired to do one set of behavioral tasks, for example: "Put the lantern in the box and close the lid." The worker is then to perform this action over and over again. The organization may or may not be concerned about what the worker feels, thinks, or wants. A simple straightforward behavioral contract is in operation here: "Do this task and the organization will reward you for your efforts, usually in the form of a paycheck." Behavioral contracts may also be used in therapy: "Do the following job-seeking tasks and you are likely to be rewarded with a job and a paycheck." Beyond assembly lines and brief behavioral contracts, both therapeutic and management tasks vary greatly in complexity.

Third, both therapist and manager are involved in setting expectations and goals. What are your goals? What do you expect? What is expected of you? The answers to these questions form the basis for determining what is to be accomplished either in therapy or in a job. Again, as in the preceding comparisons, the context and content differ for the therapist and the manager. But the process of setting goals and expectations is remarkably similar for both. The manager in a successful organization is involved in meshing the personal goals of the individual worker, the manager's goals, the goals of the organization, and relevant societal goals. If the worker cannot be helpful to the manager and the organization in meeting the organization's goals, the employment contract may be terminated. Similarly, if the manager and the organization have nothing to offer the worker in support of his or her goals, the worker is likely to sever the relationship.

In therapy the therapist and the client are involved in a similar goal-setting activity. The client contracts with the therapist to accomplish certain goals—for example, to become less depressed, to stay out of the hospital, to develop better social skills, or to work through the grief of a loss. Any of these goals could result in a therapeutic contract between therapist and client. The contract results when both the client and the therapist agree about the goal's appropriateness and feasibility.

In business organizations and in therapeutic settings there is great variability in the clarity of goals, the process by which goals are set, and the roles of the various constituencies in determining the goals to be accomplished. As the various styles of goal setting are described in this book, the similarities between processes used to accomplish the goal-setting tasks in therapy and in business will become clear.

Determining expectations is closely related to goal setting. In therapy, the expectation communicated may be "you are expected to share your intimate thoughts with me," while in business it may be "here at IBM we wear white shirts." Much of the research done on expectation setting with various pre-counseling procedures points to the importance of establishing and clarifying expectations (Hughes, 1983). Therapists sometimes encounter a client transferring his or her expectations from a medical setting to the initial clinical hour. The client may ask, "You mean you are not going to prescribe anything? You are not going to tell me what to do? Don't I need to take some medication or do something?" Clients also may bring in other preconceived expectations about therapy from the popular media. "What, you don't have a couch for me to lie on?"

Fourth, both therapist and manager are involved in determining how the goals can best be accomplished. Managers frequently possess informational, technical, and procedural expertise to help their employees arrive at decisions on how to accomplish goals. Likewise, therapists are the procedural consultants to clients who may know the changes desired but do not know how to go about attaining their goals. Like employees, clients vary in how often, how willingly, and how early in the process they consult a manager or a therapist. While some clients consult therapists early in their problem-solving process, others do so only after ignoring, rationalizing, or justifying—and then finding themselves at the end of their rope. Regardless of when in the process the therapist or manager is consulted, the client or employee is helped to reach agreed-upon goals. Frequently the goals sound simplistic. Make a profit! Feel better! Get a date! *How* these goals are reached distinguishes successful outcomes from failure. Now let us look at one type of therapy problem that is often encountered in the clinical setting.

Diane came in for therapy with a clearly stated goal. She wanted to improve her relationships with men. Most therapists would begin the therapeutic process by clarifying Diane's goal in order to obtain more information about her past relationships with men and what it was that needed improving. Armed with more information, one could approach Diane's goal in a variety of ways. For example, a therapist might try insight therapy in order to help Diane understand the early antecedents of her problems with men. Such a therapist might hypothesize that once Diane understands the reasons for her difficulties, she can work through these problems and eventually improve her interactions with men. Another therapist might decide to teach Diane some new ways of behaving around men. This treatment would be predicated on the idea that if Diane exhibited new behavior, men might respond to her differently. Another therapist might refer Diane to a social skills group where she could develop new feelings about men and new behavior toward them. Or, perhaps, a therapeutic relationship with a good male therapist might help Diane to "reprogram" old negative attitudes toward men into something more positive. Since Diane was overweight and unattractively dressed, a therapist might even decide that a good weight loss and grooming program could lead to the client's stated goal.

The first task for the therapist, then, is to develop a plan for meeting the client's goals. How the goals get met becomes the treatment plan. The therapist's role in this process parallels the manager's role in assisting those who work for him or her to develop goals and then devise plans for reaching them.

Fifth, both therapist and manager are involved in monitoring performance and evaluating progress. How do people *know* how they are doing? Are they making the expected progress? The client may say, "I'm feeling worse. Is that bad?" The therapist might respond, "No, it's good! You're finally letting some of those feelings out." Similarly, the employee might say, "Profits are down. Is that bad?" The manager might respond, "No, it's good! We need to invest in research and development for future profits." Such scenarios reflect how the therapist or manager uses a conceptual framework, looks at certain factors, and helps the client or employee to evaluate progress. As peer review and other systems for monitoring progress become more common in the field of counseling and psychotherapy, formal monitoring systems will undoubtedly be developed. Clients and employees also evaluate progress. People like to feel they are improving and meeting their goals. They may drop out of therapy or leave the job if realistic expectations about progress are not set. When a therapist and client or a manager and employee have similar goals, agree upon how to achieve them, and agree on how to evaluate progress toward them, the course of psychotherapy or business proceeds more successfully.

And sixth, both therapy and management are influenced by the nature of the therapist/client or manager/employee relationship. The relationship between client and therapist has long been recognized as affecting the outcome of many therapy contracts. The extent to which the employee is managed affects and is affected by the relationship between the manager and the employee. Workers without managerial supervision are self-managed. People who have no need of a therapeutic relationship are self-sufficient at least with regard to a formal therapy process. As the reader will see, this relationship component is one of the major dimensions of the ACT model.

There is one final and very important point to be made about the similarity between the therapeutic and managerial process. Just as within organizations managers are trained in situational leadership to base their leadership behavior on characteristics of the follower and the situation, we are suggesting that therapists make intervention decisions based on certain characteristics of the client and on the issues brought to therapy. Borrowing the key organizing concepts from situational leadership theory, we apply these principles to the field of counseling and psychotherapy. The resulting approach—adaptive counseling and therapy—integrates the contributions of the many schools and techniques of psychotherapy. Further, ACT offers a means by which successful therapists can define and explain what they are doing. Moreover, ACT offers an objective way to select an appropriate therapeutic program. When therapy reaches a stalemate because interventions do not match requirements for the most satisfactory therapeutic outcome, ACT can serve as a troubleshooting device. Because it is a model under which all psychotherapies can be subsumed, ACT can help therapists-in-training to discern the similarities and differences between various theories of psychotherapy. Finally, because it can organize all forms of therapeutic intervention, ACT serves as a valuable heuristic device that makes a number of novel predictions regarding clinical phenomena. These predictions should stimulate many research investigations in the future.

In order to make the remaining chapters in the book personally relevant for you, we urge you to respond to the twelve questions posed in Exhibit 1. These questions represent the Therapist Style Inventory (TSI). Your responses can give you feedback on several dimensions of your self-perceived therapist style from the ACT perspective. Obtaining personal feedback on your therapeutic style and effectiveness according to ACT will help to involve you in making the link between diagnosis and treatment selection that lies at the heart of ACT.

Exhibit 1. Therapist Style Inventory.

In answering the following twelve questions, assume that you are the therapist involved in the situation described. Think about what action you would choose in that situation, and then circle the response that most closely resembles the action you would take. Circle only one response to each situation. Remember to answer as you think you would if *you* were the therapist, not as you think an ideal therapist should respond. Please answer the questions in order, without spending too much time on any one situation. Do not go back over your answers or make changes.

1. As an alcoholism counselor in an inpatient treatment program, you are scheduled to meet with Ann, who has been given the assignment of identifying on a worksheet all the people who have been hurt by her alcoholism. The client arrives on time for the appointment and seems pleasant and willing to talk. After a few minutes of small talk you ask about the worksheet. She begins to explain why she has not done the assignment. You would:

   A. Say, "You have not done your assignment. We have nothing to talk about until you do."

   B. Work with her to develop the list in the session.

   C. Reflect your frustration and listen to her feelings.

   D. Ignore the missing material and ask Ann what she wants to talk about today.

2. You are in the fourth session with a fifteen-year-old who has been sent to you for truancy problems. You have established a good relationship and have just begun to focus on her school behavior. During the session the client says, "I don't really want to go to school but I'll do it for you." Your response is:

   A. "If you go to school all week, I will authorize an extra privilege."

   B. ''Good! It's important to continue your
       education, so I'm glad you'll go for me
       and for you.''
   C. ''I trust your judgment about whether
       you decide to go to school or not.''
   D. ''So you really don't want to go, but if
       you thought it would please me you would
       go.''
3. You have seen Charlie, a middle-aged man,
   two times. He has sought services voluntarily
   due to his feelings of insecurity. He recently
   was diagnosed as diabetic and has lost some
   of his vision as a result of the disease. He also
   lost his job of eighteen years due to the poor
   economy. He is happily married and has one
   son. You would:
   A. Set up a program of physical therapy in
       conjunction with his doctor and refer him
       to a competent vocational rehabilitation
       counselor.
   B. Discuss with the client his history of loss
       and begin to work out a plan with him
       on expanding his coping mechanisms.
   C. Encourage the client to express his feel-
       ings, and provide empathy and support.
   D. Make no effort to focus on his loss in
       order to avoid increasing his pain.
4. You are seeing the father of a client at the
   client's request. The client, Clint, has a history
   of emotional problems, due in part at least to
   effects of brain damage from a motorcycle accident several years ago. Clint takes medication to control some of the effects. One effect
   of the injury is that Clint occasionally has delusions that a sibling is stealing from him. Clint
   wants his father to see you so that you can con-
   vince him that Clint is telling the truth about
   the delusions. The father is an articulate, pa-

tient man who has gone through similar situations with Clint on many occasions. He understands the chronicity of his son's problems. He makes it clear that he is at the session "to keep peace" and that in the past this behavior has worked. You would:

A. Further discuss the pattern of incidents with the father in an attempt to help him express his feelings about Clint's injury and to provide the father a plan to deal with the delusion and avoid recurrent situations.

B. Express to the father your understanding of his frustrating situation and encourage him to vent any pent-up emotions.

C. Review Clint's medication with the staff psychiatrist and present recommendations to the father.

D. Allow the father to direct the course of the session.

5. You are interviewing the parents of three children. The children have been removed from the home for clear indication of child abuse. The parents were referred to you as part of the evaluation process for the court determination. They both maintain that nothing is wrong with them as individuals or as a couple. The court just has it in for them, and they want their kids back. You believe that they did abuse the children and they want the kids back to save face with the family.

A. Tell them that if they maintain the abuse they will never get their children back.

B. Indicate that cooperating in treatment with you may not only help them individually and as a couple but also improve their chances of having the children returned.

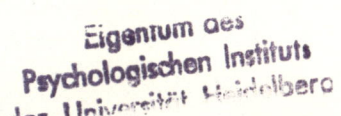

    C.   Communicate understanding of their frustration with the system and share a frustrating parenting story of your own.

    D.   Wait them out by not responding to their complaints.

6.   You are known for your work on sex roles. You have helped many women develop a more positive self-concept and take charge of their own lives. A new client, Frank, is a prominent middle-aged executive who has come to you for help in understanding his wife's problem. "She's just not like she used to be. She's gone back to school, lost twenty-five pounds of fat, and is expressing strong opinions at social gatherings." You would:

    A.   Indicate a willingness to help him look at how and why he is struggling with these changes.

    B.   Restate his feelings of confusion, anger, and threat.

    C.   Indicate that she will snap out of this phase sooner or later.

    D.   Tell him he had better look at himself and change before his wife starts looking around.

7.   Recently a case was transferred to you from another therapist who left the community. The client and the previous therapist had been working, with considerable success, on expanding social skills and social relationships. The client has expressed reluctance to get involved with a new therapist. Nevertheless, the client keeps the first scheduled appointment. During the first appointment you would:

    A.   Get a commitment from the client to continue therapy and then assign the task of meeting one new person before the next session.

    B.   Indicate your interest in the client and encourage the client to discuss the course of previous therapy.

    C.   Discuss with the client previous therapy and recent successes, and outline a new program for behavior change.

    D.   Suggest that the client terminate the therapy.

8. As part of your consultation practice, you are asked to evaluate a day-care center and provide the board of directors with recommendations. You have observed staff and children interacting and have interviewed parents individually. In addition you have reviewed the program guide for the center and compared it to state and federal guidelines, which it meets without reservation. The center has been operating for seven years with the same director. Staff turnover is low, and there is a waiting list for future openings. During your four hours of observation you did see one staff member handle a behavior problem with one of the children in a less than desirable fashion. Otherwise, indications are that the center is above satisfactory in all areas. You would:

    A.   Recommend a program on teacher effectiveness for staff members.

    B.   Meet with staff as a group and praise them for their performance overall while encouraging them to come up with a program for managing behavior problems.

    C.   Meet with staff and director to praise their work and have them outline their long-term goals.

    D.   Circulate your findings to the board and staff.

9. You have been working with a client for more than a month on her expressed unhappiness

with her current situation. Much of her content in therapy has the same theme: other people just do not understand and agree with her. You have been sharing observations and making suggestions that she seems to accept but does not apply. Not much positive change has taken place. You would:

A.   Confront her with her unwillingness to change, and use her behavior in the therapy relationship as a focus.

B.   Continue listening and reflecting.

C.   Continue listening, raise questions about her role in problem situations, but do not push.

D.   Continue to propose ways she can improve her situation, pointing out the benefits of proposed changes while appreciating her efforts in this regard.

10.   Your client, referred by a former client, states in an initial interview that recently he has been having problems going to sleep at night and feels tired all the time. He has lost interest in activities and has recurrent thoughts of death. The problems seem to have begun about two months ago, concurrently with new responsibilities at work. His brother died about this time as well. You would:

A.   Indicate a willingness to see him if he thinks he needs to talk to someone.

B.   Reinforce him for coming to see you, and recommend weekly therapy focused on reactive depression and grief.

C.   Recommend that he talk to his friends about his new problems.

D.   Recommend that he read two books, one on grief and the other on job stress. Weekly therapy sessions would focus on learning to apply the concepts to his life.

11. You are seeing an elderly retired professional woman. She recently moved from her lifelong home, several hundred miles away, to be near her youngest daughter. Her friends in the former community had all either died or moved away. She has joined two social groups and a political action group and occasionally takes group vacations. Her oldest daughter has been in and out of state institutions for the past five years and has been diagnosed as schizophrenic. Your client complains of occasionally waking up and feeling worthless and having lived her life for nothing, because of her older daughter's situation. She does not want to burden her younger daughter, who has no sympathy for her sister's situation. She and the younger daughter have a good relationship otherwise. Your client gets tearful during sessions when discussing her older daughter. You would:

   A. Refer her to an older adult group and give her reading material on the aging process.

   B. Tell her that these feelings of worthlessness are quite common complaints of the elderly.

   C. Indicate your understanding of her feelings, and allow her to talk about her daughter in a nonjudgmental atmosphere.

   D. Encourage her to examine her life for positive relationships, and work with her on a plan to expand her self-worth through volunteer work.

12. You have been seeing this client for several months. Treatment has centered on improving the quality of his relationships with co-workers. He has accepted and applied insights

gained during the sessions most satisfactorily.
During the current session he suggests ter-
minating the therapy. You would:
A.   Allow him to make that decision.
B.   Tell him to prepare a list of benefits he
     believes he has gained for review in the
     next session.
C.   Praise him for meeting the goals of his
     current therapy contract, reviewing the
     specific goals as you do so.
D.   Share with him your feelings about his
     progress in therapy.

Since we believe it is more useful to read about the ACT
model before scoring your inventory, we describe adaptive
counseling and therapy in Chapters Two and Three. These
chapters will help you to understand the meaning of your TSI
scores. We will show you how to score your responses in Chapter
Four.

2

▦ ▦ ▦ ▦ ▦ ▦ ▦ ▦ ▦ ▦ ▦ ▦ ▦

Components of
the ACT Model

In order to understand adaptive counseling and therapy, it is
first necessry to understand situational leadership (Hersey and
Blanchard, 1977), the management theory that forms the basis
of ACT. This chapter describes situational leadership theory
in detail and then translates its constructs into a theory for psychotherapy that provides an organizing framework for the eclectic approach to counseling. Before discussing situational leadership, however, we return to the case of James that opened
Chapter One.

James, as you may recall, only dabbled at employment
and graduate school and in other numerous ways demonstrated
a general lack of responsible behavior. James's therapist, whom
we will call Millie, was well respected by both colleagues and
clients. She was most comfortable using a client-centered,
insight-oriented, psychodynamic combination of therapy. James
had been referred by a friend who had recently completed successful counseling with Millie. Millie hoped for a good therapeutic relationship with James—one in which he would, through
trust, be able to share a lot about himself and, through self-
understanding, eventually make necessary and growthful
changes.

The first clinical problem Millie encountered was motivating James to attend his therapy sessions with regularity and
arrive on time. Eventually James improved in attendance and

punctuality, although his approach to therapy was reminiscent of his approach to graduate school. There was a certain respectability in saying he was going to counseling, and James could hide behind the respectability conferred by this apparent attempt at growth, education, and change. Therapy, like school, enabled him to avoid more odious responsibilities.

After about three months, James was not only willing to come for therapy, he began to rather enjoy spending an hour talking about himself. Millie was an understanding therapist, and unlike James's wife she did not badger him to *do* anything other than talk and share. The difficulty with the therapy was that James was not making any substantive changes in the behavior that was so problematic. He did not finish his dissertation. He did not get a steady job. He did not change any of his promiscuous sexual behavior. He did not give up his drug habit. After two years of therapy and no change on the home front, James's wife filed for divorce. After the divorce, James withdrew from his parental responsibilities. Moreover, his attendance in counseling became less predictable. Within two months he had totally drifted away from the therapy process. He did not complete his dissertation in the allotted time period. As of this writing, James is unemployed most of the winter and works as a house painter during the summer. He still sporadically attends classes that interest him.

What went wrong with James's therapy? Was he such a hopeless client that no treatment would have been helpful in changing his problematic behavior? We think not! Rather, we believe (as many of you reading this may also believe) that the particular treatment approach which Millie applied to James was not the appropriate treatment to make a difference in his life. Before we learned about situational leadership and began applying its constructs to therapy, we, like many of you, intuitively would have made a different choice for James's treatment than Millie made. But we would not have understood exactly what went into that choice. ACT provides direction for the problem of *which* treatment and *which* therapist style to use with a client.

James's therapy was, first of all, ineffective. Secondly, James's wife's ultimatum, once the ''stick'' that motivated him, was no longer a prod for therapy. James discontinued treatment. The problem of continuation in psychotherapy is closely akin to the problem of ineffective therapy. In the one case the client fails to improve because the treatment does not work. In the other case the client fails to improve because he or she drops out of therapy.

Garfield (1980) notes that significant numbers of clients who evidence a need for therapy simply drop out after several sessions. One study that analyzed more than 1,000 cases (Garfield and Kurtz, 1974) showed that of 560 clients receiving psychoanalytically oriented therapy, 43 percent dropped out of treatment before the fifth interview. We hypothesize that the culprit in both ineffective and prematurely terminated therapy is the application of the wrong treatment plan and therapist style for the client. As we describe adaptive counseling and therapy as a model for understanding psychotherapeutic eclecticism, we will illustrate how the application of ACT can solve the problems of ineffective and prematurely terminated therapy.

Situational Leadership and ACT

Much of ACT represents a straightforward adaptation of Paul Hersey's and Kenneth Blanchard's situational leadership theory to the practice of psychotherapy. Hersey and Blanchard (1977) emphasize the maximum use of human resources in organizations through the exercise of appropriate leadership style by managers. For them, leadership style should be determined by the task-relevant maturity of the manager's subordinates. They hypothesize that a curvilinear relationship exists among the variables of leader task behavior, leader relationship behavior, and subordinate's maturity.

ACT uses these same three variables, which we have renamed the therapist's directive behavior, the therapist's supportive behavior, and the client's readiness for the therapeutic task. In other words, we are suggesting that the best therapist style can be determined by assessing the client's readiness on the therapeutic task under consideration and then applying the appropriate therapist directive behavior and therapist supportive behavior. We are hypothesizing that the same curvilinear relationship among the variables exists in ACT as in situational leadership. To understand how ACT works, we must first fully understand the three basic components of ACT: the therapist's directive behavior and supportive behavior, the client's task readiness, and the match between the two.

Therapist Behavior

A commonly accepted definition of leadership is "the process of influencing the activities of individual or group efforts toward goal achievement in a given situation" (Hersey and Blanchard, 1977, p. 84). Clearly, this is also a description of what therapists do. As we discussed in Chapter One, ACT presumes that the roles of leader and therapist are somewhat comparable and therefore draws heavily from research on leadership behavior. The therapist, like the manager, is usually the designated leader. Sometimes, of course, a client can lead a therapist or a subordinate can lead a manager. Although neither leadership behavior nor therapist behavior is role-bound, both client and therapist, like subordinate and manager, need to be aware whenever a role reversal is in effect. Otherwise confusion and inefficiency may result.

Studies consistently have found two principal components of the leadership process: one has to do with the amount of emphasis placed on getting the job done or the goals met; the other has to do with the relationship between the leader and the follower (Stogdill and Coorn, 1957; Blake and Mouton, 1964; Hersey and Blanchard, 1977; Blanchard and Johnson, 1982). ACT uses these two dimensions to describe a therapist's behavior. In the ACT psychotherapy model, these two dimensions are referred to as therapist directive behavior and therapist supportive behavior.

Directive Behavior. Behavior focused on the accomplishment of an identified goal is on the *directive* continuum of therapist behavior. The questions "what?", "when?", "where?", "in what order?", "by what means?", and "who does what?" all need to be answered on the directive continuum. The variation lies in how much structure or direction is provided by the therapist and how much by the client or other sources. The therapist who is operating high on the directive dimension would be focused on accomplishing a specific task, initiating activities with clients, and providing a specific structure for the accomplishment of those activities. On the other hand, the therapist who is operating low on the directive dimension would be less goal-oriented and would look to the client for structure and direction in the clinical meeting. It is not difficult to see that a behavioral approach is high on the directive dimension while the psychoanalytic approach is considered low.

High-directive therapists are not necessarily interested only in overt behavior. Nor are low-directive therapists interested only in cognitions and feelings. It is in fact possible to address thoughts and emotions by using a high-directive style. Rational-emotive therapy (Ellis and Grieger, 1977) is a good example of a high-directive therapy that also addresses thoughts and feelings. The important point is that the directive level of a given technique depends upon the degree to which the initiation and structuring of activities are controlled by the therapist (high-directive) or the client (low-directive).

Sometimes it is the setting in which counseling takes place, rather than just the therapist or the client, that determines the structure. Clients who voluntarily enter a behavioral drug treatment program, a stop smoking clinic, or a weight control clinic may be directing themselves into a highly structured, and therefore a high-directive, situation. Patients who are involuntarily committed to a psychiatric treatment facility may have the high-directive situation imposed upon them. Patients who participate in psychoanalysis are generally in a low-directive setting. Although some settings provide more direction than others by their very nature, settings differ in the amount of direction or structure they impose. Even penal institutions and state psychiatric hospitals, for example, vary among themselves regarding directiveness. Our client James is in a nonstructured, low-directive, outpatient psychotherapy setting. Yet not all outpatient psychotherapy is low on the directive dimension. The role of the setting, or what we will call the form of treatment in ACT, is discussed in detail in Chapter Five.

Supportive Behavior. A second, independent continuum along which a therapist's style may be measured is the degree of support or relationship behavior. The importance of the therapist/client relationship has long been appreciated in psychotherapy. Initially, analytic theorists conceived the client/therapist relationship as being central to the working through of the transference neurosis. Later, client-centered therapists viewed the therapeutic relationship as necessary and sufficient to produce therapeutic change. While therapy generally implies some client/therapist relationship, there are some conditions in therapy under which the quality of the therapeutic relationship is decidedly secondary. Setting up and running a token economy program would be one example.

Therapists high on the supportive behavior dimension—for example, client-centered therapists—would devote considerable time, thought, and energy to showing concern for the client, demonstrating support, being empathic, and building rapport. Such techniques are designed to help clients feel understood, approved of, cared for, and supported by the therapist. Techniques that do not include facilitating the therapeutic relationship would be classified as low on the supportive behavior continuum. Behaviorism and certain aspects of the cognitive therapies demonstrate low-supportive therapeutic strategies.

Classifying an approach as high or low in supportive behavior does not imply that one results in a better therapeutic situation than the other. In fact, ACT predicts that the best therapeutic situations are the results of accurately assessing the client's readiness pertaining to a specific goal of therapy and correctly determining the treatment most likely to help the client meet that goal. Two considerations in the selection of a treatment are how much directive and how much supportive behavior will be required of the therapist.

Nearly every practicing therapist has been in the puzzling position of using good relationship skills but noting no behavior change in certain clients. As you will see, this is one of the major problems in the case of James. In certain situations, the use of a high-supportive behavior approach will lead to a poor therapeutic relationship, whereas the choice of a low-supportive style is more likely to yield a good working alliance. This phenomenon is observable when a client, after talking nonstop during the initial hours of therapy, says, "I feel so much better. Just talking about this problem has been helpful." Clearly, in this initial hour there cannot be much of a relationship between therapist and client. In fact, too much input from the therapist might have impeded the client's ability to express himself or herself, and the catharsis appears to have been the therapeutic agent rather than the therapist/client relationship. Similarly, there are times in every therapist's professional life when he or she needs to be saying: "It doesn't matter whether you like me or not. What does matter is that you stop drinking (or stealing, or abusing your children, or exposing yourself, and so forth).

One clearly psychotic client, who was referred to therapy by his supervisor for continually espousing a belief that he was Jesus, was seen only twice by his counselor. The therapist refused to be sidetracked from the immediate task of therapy, which was to help the client maintain his job. She did not spend several sessions developing her relationship with the client. She did not attempt to cure his delusions or to delve into his history in order to understand his psychosis. Instead, she simply worked with him to develop strategies for keeping his mouth shut about his delusion on the job. Two years later, he was still employed in the same custodial position. The functional stability of his job was critical to his well-being. In the matter of relationship behavior, ACT's objective is to define the parameters for using both high- and low-supportive behavior in a therapeutic context.

Therapist Styles

The two dimensions of therapist behavior, direction and support, can now be combined to produce the four basic therapist behavior quadrants presented in Figure 1. Each of these quadrants depicts a different therapist style. Each style, in turn, represents a different mix of the directive and supportive dimensions. The styles are labeled S1 through S4. As we will see in

Figure 1. Therapist Styles.

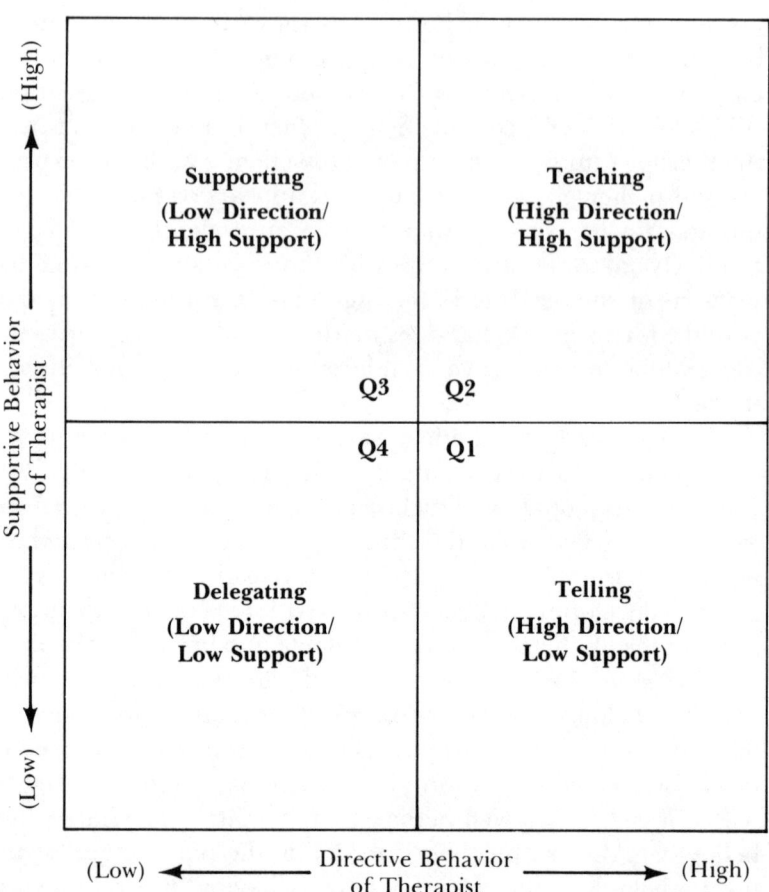

Chapter Three, specific therapeutic techniques can be assigned to each of these four categories. We should also point out that techniques relating to a particular theoretical school of thought can be assigned to an appropriate quadrant.

The four quadrants in Figure 1 are designated Q1 through Q4. The ACT model refers to the four quadrants as Q1 (telling), Q2 (teaching), Q3 (supporting), and Q4 (delegating). The different styles (S1 through S4) associated with each of the quadrants are elaborated below. We will describe the therapist style within each quadrant as if the therapist's behavior on the support and behavior dimensions rested in some static spot. Remember, however, that directive behavior and supportive behavior lie on a continuum and that therefore a therapist using behaviors in one area of a quadrant would be using somewhat different behaviors than a therapist using behaviors from a different point within that quadrant.

S1: High Direction/Low Support (HD/LS). At the extreme end of the *telling* style, the therapist is in charge of the therapy goals. He or she assumes responsibility for deciding what needs to be done, how it needs to be done, in what order, and so on. The client's role is to comply—to do what is prescribed. Medically, this style can be seen in the practice of emergency room medicine in which the patient is essentially passive while the physician diagnoses the problem and implements the treatment. Essential to operating from the extreme corner of this quadrant in therapy is an assessment which indicates that the client is not in a position, whether owing to ignorance or to emotional disturbance, to make appropriate therapeutic, and perhaps even life, decisions.

In psychotherapy, when it becomes clear that a client is either unwilling or unable or both to direct himself toward goal achievement, most therapists instinctively move toward a more directive stance with that client. If they do not, therapy may grind to a halt. To continue to require autonomous functioning from a client unable to function in this manner is to ask the impossible. One does not ask a person in the midst of a psychotic break to decide whether or not to go to the hospital. Such a person is unable to make appropriate decisions. Similarly, one does not ask court-ordered clients whether or not they want to continue treatment. It is unlikely that these clients are internally motivated for psychotherapy. Frequently, for example, in confrontive treatment for substance abuse, one leans strongly on the resistant abuser to accept some form of heavily structured treatment. Returning to James's case for a moment, we can see that his wife applied a strong dose of Q1 to motivate him to go to counseling. In essence, James's wife said: "If you want this marriage to continue, you will get help.'' Based on James's history, it is doubtful that a less direct pressure would have been successful in motivating him to begin counseling.

In order for a therapist to be able to use an S1 style effectively, he or she must have a power base from which to operate. In essence, the counselor must have some control over carrots and sticks for the client. The client may directly transfer power to the therapist either because of the client's assessment that sticks and carrots are necessary or because of the therapist's presumed expertise. Sometimes the power is transferred to the therapist from an outside source—through the ultimatum of a family member, for example, as it was in James's case, or perhaps in the form of an employer's directive or a court order. The role of the therapist's power in therapy is discussed in Chapter Seven.

Quadrants 1 and 4 are the quadrants within which therapies low in therapist supportive behavior are grouped. Remember that low is a relative term—that is, S1 and S4 therapy is low on support compared with S2 or S3 therapy. Except for some of the crisis situations described earlier, there is almost always some element of support in psychotherapy.

S2: High Direction/High Support (HD/HS). ACT calls this quadrant *teaching*. The teaching role is one of dispensing information and skill training to persons who need them and who, for the most part, have indicated their willingness to learn. The client who is best approached with an S2 therapist style is a client who is motivated or willing but lacks the skills, the understanding, the ability, or the confidence to change.

Many of us look back on our school careers and recall that the teachers who most inspired us were those who provided information along with a good dose of enthusiasm and encouragement. The best teachers often were the ones who took a personal interest in us and seemed to care that we learned the material. Counselors using the S2 approach are much like these inspiring teachers. In psychotherapy, it is common knowledge that change of any kind is difficult. Suppose, for example, we are faced with a client who is meek and victimized by other people. Suppose also that this person wishes to alter the situation. In order to maximize the opportunity for change to occur, most therapists would combine the teaching of assertion skills with some form of encouragement and support. They would, in effect, take an S2 stance with that client. Similarly, much sexual counseling requires giving the client new information related to sexuality in the context of a supportive client/therapist relationship. The therapist is the teacher; the client is the student— gaining information about new sexual behavior. If therapy succeeds, the client will gain new confidence and understanding of his or her sexuality, take this new learning into real life, and practice new sexual behavior.

S3: Low Direction/High Support (LD/HS). A therapist's behavior in this style is primarily *supporting*. The focus is less on what the client is doing and more on *how* the client is doing. The therapist may give hints, suggestions, or reminders of previously learned concepts but is more concerned with providing care, support, and understanding. An S3 image that comes to mind is that of a football coach during an important game. Teaching technique is reserved for practice sessions. During the game the coach supports his players. He is intensely involved with how players on the field are doing—pacing up and down the sidelines, slapping backs, shouting encouragement, cheering for triumph, commiserating with failure, making suggestions, and reminding the players of particular strategies. Clinical examples of S3 abound, as it is often the most natural stance for a therapist to take and is frequently the style taught in graduate programs. Physically comforting a client who is newly bereaved or allowing a client to share his joy are both examples of S3 behavior. In this quadrant, the therapist has moved away from both telling and teaching. In short, responsibility for structure and direction belongs to the client. The therapist listens, empathizes, facilitates, clarifies, and reflects material presented by the client. Rogerian therapy is the prototype of this high-support/low-direction position.

S4: Low Direction/Low Support (LD/LS). In the S4 quadrant, *delegating*, the therapist functions mostly as an interested observer of the client's progress. The prototype of S4 therapist behavior is classic psychoanalysis in which the client is fully responsible for content and the analyst serves as a clarifier-commentator. Presumably the client is both willing and able to direct his or her own process.

By now, it may be obvious that quadrants representing S1 to S4 can also serve as an analogue of the therapy process itself. It is not unusual for treatment to move from a therapist position of more control (usually seen in the early phases) to a therapist position of less control (usually used in the last phases), depending upon the assessed needs of the client. The S4 position is generally the position of choice in the termination phase of successful therapy of all kinds. As the client achieves objectives and gains confidence in his or her ability to self-direct, it is most appropriate that the therapist relinquish control and abandon a heavily supportive or heavily directive approach. Such clients are capable of providing support and direction for themselves.

Relationship of Client Readiness to Therapeutic Style

The heart of ACT lies in the prediction that the effectiveness of the four categories of therapist styles (S1 to S4) depends on the client's task readiness. This section discusses the concept of client readiness level. We will also comment on the application of the most appropriate therapist style based on the client's readiness level and speculate about the results of misalignment between therapist style and client readiness.

A client's readiness for therapy is similar to a child's readiness for learning. One of its significant components is motivation (Brammer and Shostrom, 1977). In ACT, readiness is not to be understood as a global personality trait that an individual exhibits in all situations. Readiness for ACT purposes is relative to a cluster of closely related activities or tasks. Consider, for a moment, the stereotype of the dedicated, brilliant scientist who is a social isolate. How task-ready is this person? It depends entirely on the context in which the scientist is being evaluated. It depends on what task she must be ready to do.

Work-related readiness could be extremely high, while social and interpersonal readiness could be quite low. Exactly the opposite readiness profile would exist for the socially active, interpersonally skilled student who cannot manage to attend classes regularly or complete her assignments on time. In summary, it is important not to consider a client ready or unready in some global sense. It is also necessary not to see client readiness as a personality construct. ACT recommends that the concept of readiness be considered only with respect to each of the objectives targeted for therapy and to the related tasks to be performed.

Three Elements of Client Readiness. Just as therapist styles are divided into four quadrants, so too are client readiness levels: R1 is low readiness, R2 is low moderate readiness, R3 is high moderate readiness, and R4 is high readiness. In ACT (as in situational leadership), the three aspects of client readiness are willingness (motivation), ability (competence), and self-confidence. These three elements are used in ACT for assessing client readiness in order to determine the therapy style that will be most effective. Willingness, ability, and self-confidence in various combinations constitute the four levels of client readiness.

Clients who are both unwilling and unable, or who lack the self-confidence, to accomplish the targeted clinical goal are in the low-readiness (R1) category. Those who are willing, able, and confident enough to make necessary changes are in the high-readiness (R4) quadrant. Individuals with mixed or intermediate levels of willingness, ability, and confidence generally can be assigned to the middle quadrants (R2 and R3). It is important to reiterate that these categories are defined discretely for convenience and clarity. In practice, there is fluidity and movement from one quadrant to another with respect to the tasks on which the client's readiness level is being assessed.

We return now to our discussion of the case of James and examine these three aspects of his readiness level as related to specific therapeutic tasks. As in most therapeutic situations, the therapist's initial task is to establish a relationship with the client. Millie, James's therapist, wanted to establish a relationship with James that would lead to a commitment to counseling on his part and to an eventual change in his problematic behavior. However, in the early phase of therapy, we know that James is not very committed to a clinical process. Rather, he is attending his therapy sessions because his wife has given him an ultimatum. James is unwilling, although in all probability able, to engage in therapy. We have no information about his confidence level. Whether or not James believes he can successfully use therapy is unknown. It does seem clear, however, that without a very directive stance by his wife he would not be in treatment. The direction for being in therapy comes from James's wife and the necessary support for engaging in therapy is supplied by Millie, the therapist.

There are several other therapeutic tasks or goals we can identify with the meager information available to us. What we do not know is whether these goals belong to the therapist, to James, to James's wife, or to some combination of these people. Therapeutic goals might include:

- Finish school or officially withdraw.
- Find a job that has some longevity and can help to support the family.
- Give up his promiscuous sexual activity.
- Give up drugs and alcohol.

The therapist can use several methods for discovering a client's willingness, ability, and confidence level related to therapeutic tasks. She can ask the client directly. She can gather data about current behavior through observation, questioning, assessment, or outside sources. Or she can evaluate reactions and behavioral responses to suggestions and assignments related to specific therapeutic tasks. Using our knowledge of James's case, we can determine where James falls on each of the specified therapeutic tasks.

James definitely had the ability to complete graduate school, although he was not very confident about his ability to do so. His motivation to complete his degree was mixed. On the one hand, the success of completion was appealing. On the other hand, once he completed school, James would have no excuse for not finding permanent employment.

The lack of motivation to complete graduate school was directly related to James's readiness on the second therapeutic goal. James was unwilling to find permanent employment. He actually preferred doing odd jobs and did not want the responsibility of a full-time job. Because he was intelligent, presented himself well, and possessed several desirable skills in carpentry and painting, James had the ability to find steady work. He was reasonably confident that if he wanted a full-time job, he would be able to get one.

James was definitely unwilling to give up his sexual pursuits. As it turned out, both he and his wife had been involved in extramarital sexual activity including multicouple sex and mate swapping. This was, therefore, not an activity that was particularly disturbing to either husband or wife. While no doubt James had the ability to give up sexual promiscuity and infidelity, he had no motivation to do so.

And, finally, as is often the case, James had little sense of the impact of his substance abuse on the various aspects of his life. He was aware of other problems in his life but dealt with them through the coping mechanism of chemical dependency. He was totally unable to see that his substance abuse was *creating* some of the other problems in his life. James was neither willing nor able to work on his drug and alcohol habits.

The Concept of Match and Move. ACT conceptualizes progress in therapy as a developmental process. Successful therapy is the movement by the client from a less ready state to a more ready state in terms of accomplishing a designated therapeutic task. This maturation process can also be viewed as movement from a passive to a more active stance or as a gradual shift from a dependent to an independent position. As a general rule, clients tend to rely more heavily upon the therapist for direction and support early in the therapeutic process than in the termination phase of treatment.

It cannot be overemphasized that assessment of a client's readiness level is critical to determining what therapeutic approach will be most beneficial for that client. The optimal approach will not only meet the client's needs at his or her present readiness level but will also encourage movement by the client to a higher readiness level. Implicit in the ACT model is the notion that a miscalculation of client readiness in either direction will decrease the chances of therapeutic progress and perhaps even undermine the process. With clients at a low readiness level, a great deal of direction behavior by the therapist is needed in order to initiate movement in therapy. It is precisely for this reason that highly directive techniques are often successful with severely disturbed or poorly functioning clients. As the client becomes more willing, able, and confident, the therapist reduces directiveness and takes a mostly supportive stance with the client. Once substantial readiness is achieved, the therapist may reduce support and encouragement until the client is functioning independently. Independent functioning is a sign of readiness to work on a new therapeutic goal or to terminate treatment.

Employing a schema similar to Hersey and Blanchard (1977), we can depict the relationship between client readiness level and recommended style as in Figure 2. (This relationship is discussed more thoroughly in Chapter Five.) One can see the four quadrants depicting the four therapist styles as shown in Figure 1. The curve, which represents a continuum of therapist behavior, is actually the smoothing of a stepwise process of decreasing direction and increasing support through S1 and S2. For S3 and S4 the curve is a smoothed stepwise process of reducing both direction and support as the client assumes more and more responsibility for maintaining the targeted therapeutic behaviors. The characteristics of client readiness are listed in the appropriate quadrant in Figure 2. The most effective therapist style is the style described in the quadrant in which the client's assessed readiness is listed. Details on how to assess the client's readiness level will be discussed in Chapter Five.

Using this method, we can now determine an appropriate therapeutic style for James related to each of the therapeutic tasks we have discussed. In terms of James's commitment to therapy, we know that he is able to participate in the process, but he is not very motivated. This determination that James is somewhat unwilling although able to participate in a therapy process suggests that James is a high R1 or low R2 on this

Figure 2. Effective Therapist Styles.

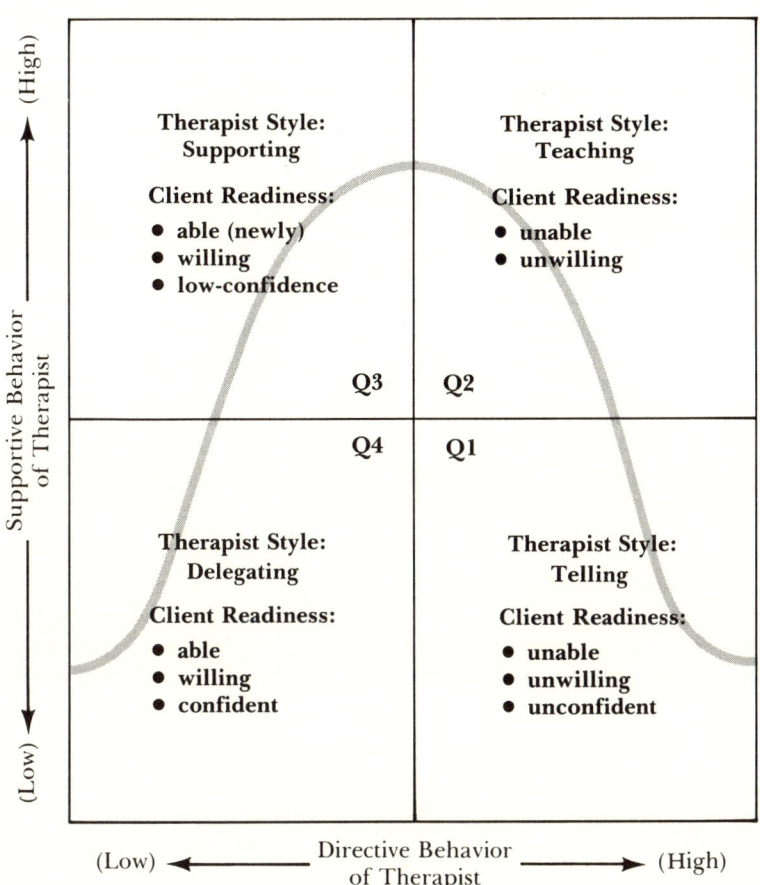

therapeutic task. Consequently, as we take the vertical line and intersect the curve, we find that what James needs in order to gain commitment for therapy is high direction and medium support. Who will provide this? Translated therapeutically, Millie would probably have to give James specific instructions related to attendance to therapy while at the same time listening, empathizing, and understanding with some intentionality. Since James's wife is insisting on therapy, however, the direction is already being provided. In this early phase of therapy, Millie must match her supportive behavior to his performance on the task. Regular and punctual attendance would be noticed and appreciated. If James missed a session or arrived late, he would be greeted with something like: "James, I expect you to be here every Tuesday at 10:30. If an emergency prevents your being here, please give me a call. Otherwise, you will be charged for the hour." He would not be told: "The therapy is for you. You can decide if you want to be here or not." The high-structure/medium-relationship approach is directly related to the task of commitment to therapy, but it can also help James to develop more responsible behavior. The focus on responsibility will later be helpful in achieving his other therapeutic goals.

A similar therapeutic scenario can be established for the goal of finishing school. James's lack of clear motivation and his lack of confidence suggest that he is going to need a great deal of help in structuring his time and energy if he is to complete his dissertation on time. Since the therapist feels certain that James has the ability to complete school, she does not have to worry about setting an impossible goal for him. Specific short and attainable assignments need to be established. "Bring me two pages on the review of the literature for your dissertation next Tuesday." Moreover, a reward system for celebrating success related to accomplishment needs to be identified. James's lack of confidence in his ability to finish his schoolwork on time suggests that he will need significant support from Millie. "Great, James. These two pages cover several references. You must have done significant reading this week. I hope you feel as proud of yourself as I do." This support serves as part of the reward system. On this therapeutic task, then, Millie needs to provide high direction and moderate to high support—an S2 orientation.

The employment problem is of a slightly different nature. Since James is totally unmotivated but has both the capacity and the confidence to find permanent work, the therapist and the client may first need to determine whether the goal of permanent employment should even be part of the therapeutic contract. The external influence of James's wife may be one factor in this determination. If James agrees to this goal, he will be agreeing to have the therapist provide the structure and direction that he cannot provide for himself. In this case, therapy around an employment goal would involve specific structured assignments from the therapist. "I expect you to read the want ads this week and check the university job board. Select at least three jobs that you can handle and send your résumé and an inquiry letter to each of these prospective employers. I'd like to see your résumé and a copy of the letters next week." This is mostly an S1 approach with occasional dashes of S2. Increased support can be provided as James progresses toward this goal.

If James does not agree to the goal of finding permanent work, the therapeutic task becomes one of determining a different and more acceptable employment goal. Presumably James is both willing and able to focus on the task of finding a suitable employment goal. Therefore, a supportive style of counseling—S3—can be used with more or less direction as the situation requires. The therapist would want to help James explore not only where he hopes to go in terms of employment but also some of the antecedents that have shaped his beliefs and feelings about the world of work. Keep in mind that confrontation is a valuable aspect of support. In addition to all the positive supportive behavior, by this time Millie has enough of a relationship with James to confront him supportively when necessary. "I understand that you hate the idea of regular work, James, but tell me how the family is going to meet all its financial obligations with you bringing in part-time wages." Such a statement is not inconsistent with an S3 therapist stance.

Philandering will probably not be a behavior that James is going to work on in therapy. With the additional history about the marital contract related to extramarital sex, it is clear that a goal of sexual fidelity would be unwarranted, at least at this time. The wife's distress—and therefore the marital issues that forced James into treatment in the first place—would appear to be related to other areas of problematic behavior.

Treating the substance abuse is a tougher problem than the other goals because the client may be unwilling and unable to abandon his habits whereas the therapist and the environment have assessed that drugs and alcohol are impairing progress in other essential aspects of his life. In this event, the goal of tackling the substance abuse is one in which James is a clear R1. He needs a great deal of direction in working on this problem. This direction may be in the form of an auxiliary substance abuse program, attendance at AA or NA, or highly structured work with Millie. ''Keep track of everything you take this week.'' Or ''I want you to go through one day entirely clean this week.'' Whatever the treatment, it must be highly structured because James lacks both the motivation and the ability to help himself.

As we mentioned earlier in this chapter, in order for a therapist to take an S1 stance effectively, he or she must have the power to do so. In James's case, the power is transferred to the therapist through the wife. It is the wife's ultimatum to James, and his desire to maintain the marriage, that gives the therapist permission to tell James what to do. It is not unusual in the treatment of chemical dependency for the power behind an S1 stance to emanate from a source external to the therapist and the client—the courts, family members, the employer, and so forth. If neither the therapist nor anyone else has the power to force treatment issues, the prognosis for sustained treatment is poor. More will be said about the role of power in therapy in Chapter Seven.

As James begins to make progress on the therapeutic goals, his willingness and motivation will no doubt change. Remember that over the course of therapy, the counselor is moving along the curve with the client so that the treatment approach is always synchronized with the client's task readiness. This movement on the part of the client, which is a sign of progress, highlights the importance to the counselor of having a range of counseling styles. Moreover, we think you can appreciate the value of range, flexibility, and adaptability on the part of a therapist since clients are typically working on more than one therapeutic issue at a time and are at different readiness levels for different tasks.

The Probable Success of a Therapy Style

The appropriate therapist style for each readiness level is shown in Figure 2. ACT not only predicts the optimal therapy style for each readiness level but also suggests the probability of success for the other three therapist styles when applied to that situation. As in situational leadership theory, each style's probable success depends on its distance from the predicted "best style" along the bell-shaped curve. Styles at a greater distance stand less of a chance of success than styles nearer to the recommended therapist style for that readiness level. Table 1 represents an ordering in terms of probability of success of the four therapist styles at each of the four client readiness levels.

Table 1. Rank Ordering of Probable Success of Therapist Styles.

Client's Readiness Level	High Probability of Success	Intermediate Probability of Success	Low Probability of Success
Low	Telling	Teaching > Supporting	Delegating
Low moderate	Teaching	Supporting = Telling	Delegating
High moderate	Supporting	Delegating = Teaching	Telling
High	Delegating	Supporting > Teaching	Telling

Note that supporting and teaching therapist styles (styles that include strong relationship behavior) are never designated as having a low probability for success. While they are not always the optimal approaches, they can be considered somewhat safe in that they will never be the least preferred approach. Being totally unsure about a client's readiness level, one cannot go far wrong by employing a style that is strong in relationship behavior. In the absence of other information, therapists characteristically engage in moderate amounts of supportive behavior while seeking information on which to formulate an approach to treatment. One should not, however, simply choose a style that avoids gross mismatches of therapist style and the client's task readiness. Such an approach would be far from the precise selection and matching we hope the ACT model will foster.

You now have been introduced to all the components of ACT. The remaining chapters of this book expand on the ACT model presented in this chapter, explore the implications of using the ACT model, and elucidate the model through the use of case material. ACT is an applied model for therapy. Much of the empirical literature, theoretical insight, and practical wisdom developed over the years in the field of psychotherapy will be reinterpreted from the ACT perspective.

3

Using the ACT Model with Major Therapeutic Approaches

Those who are on the front lines actually doing counseling and psychotherapy usually do not spend their time arguing about the best theoretical approach for helping their clients. Their clinical work has suggested to them that different clients and their different problems require different kinds of therapy. It seems likely that the everyday practice of psychotherapy has led to the rise in eclecticism described in Chapter One. An eclectic approach to psychotherapy would not be possible, however, if there were not a variety of theoretical schools of counseling from which to choose. This chapter examines our understanding of how some of the various theories of psychotherapy developed, how the development of these diverse schools is consistent with ACT theory, and how each approach to therapy can be selectively used as a treatment tool by the systematically eclectic practitioner.

Historically, there have been differing opinions about which therapy is "best." If we examine the various theories of psychotherapy from an ACT perspective, we see that each of the major approaches is "right" when the client's task readiness is taken into account. In other words, it seems likely that the interactions of therapist and client which first gave rise to a theoretical perspective did so because there was a match between the therapy tasks, the client's readiness level related to those tasks, and the therapist's approach. We would further contend that therapists who remain wedded to one particular theoretical persuasion have probably experienced success using that approach and the success can probably be traced to the client variables we are discussing here. A major process at work in psychotherapy has been different theorists and clinicians working with clients of differing competence, confidence, and motivation. Out of their work came loyalty to a range of conceptual models and guidelines for how a therapist should behave. We would also suggest that the current rise in eclecticism is tied to the fact that therapists who are treating a broad range of clients are not finding one approach to be sufficient.

If indeed we believe that each theory about human behavior was the result of a theorist looking at a specific population, it is evident that creative theorists in psychotherapy were faced with the task of finding a therapy to fit the problems with which their clients coped. As each theorist or school of theorists develops an appropriate therapeutic model based on the research client population, the presentation of the new model to the clinical world is much like the metaphorical problem of a group fitting a mosaic together, each piece of which is designed by an individual worker. Sometimes when a person brings a piece to be fitted into the mosaic, other members of the group exclude it by saying, "Doesn't fit." "Not in our area you don't." "We already have one." This resistance to the introduction of new ideas can also be seen in the therapeutic community. Perhaps this resistance is not so much a matter of defensiveness, but rather a problem of fit—the resister's recognition that a particular theory really will not work with the population in question. At other times, a person may produce an extremely fine mosaic piece that is well received by the other workers. When everyone likes a particular piece, it is stretched to cover more and more of the mosaic, frequently ruining the original design. In therapy, too, we have been guilty of taking effective models for change and stretching them until they weaken or break what was originally a valuable, but limited, contribution to the total picture of human behavior.

Adaptive counseling and therapy is not a replacement for theories of human behavior. In fact, it is dependent on the full range of theory and technique available to the practitioner. With this in mind, the remainder of the chapter will look at some specific schools of psychotherapy and explain how each of them fits into the ACT model. We will begin by looking at the four ACT quadrants and placing various therapies in the appropriate squares. Since adaptive counseling and therapy is primarily concerned with how therapists behave and how they select from a range of therapeutic interventions to match the client's readiness, this discussion will pay particular attention to the client's readiness and the therapist's behavior on the directive and supportive dimensions. We are limiting this discussion to conceptual models of therapy and will not comment on specific techniques.

Psychoanalysis: A Style 4 Approach

Freud's psychoanalytic therapy developed as the result of research. The original population studied and treated by Freud considerably determined the direction of his theoretical contributions. Psychoneurotic disorders such as hysteria, obsession-compulsion, and other states primarily characterized by anxiety are the disorders out of which psychoanalytic treatment emerged and the ones for which this particular psychotherapy is best suited. Most of Freud's patients were bright, verbal, and in sufficient daily pain to be willing to invest heavily in treatment in order to achieve some relief.

Psychoanalysis, because of its somewhat distant style of therapist behavior, requires a highly motivated and capable client. What other kind of person would be willing to commit three or four hours a week for two to five years, not to mention thousands of dollars, to a process of introspection and detailed self-examination? Contemporary parodies of classic analysis as in some of Woody Allen's films exaggerate this motivated and capable patient. Allen humorously depicts himself stretched out on the analyst's couch, painfully but articulately recalling the details of some childhood trauma—a trauma that was frequently sexual in nature. It is not entirely coincidental that many celebrities have revealed personal excursions into long-term psychoanalytic treatment. Such people certainly have the wherewithal for this type of psychotherapy. In the case of actors and actresses, it is almost a professional requirement to be able to search one's soul and dig deep psychologically. Descending into one's own psyche is not unlike immersing oneself into the heart and soul of a stage character. Psychotherapists and psychologically minded lay people comprise another large segment of those who have invested in psychoanalysis. All of this is consistent with the requirement that analysands have considerable motivation and the ability to participate in a long-term, self-directed process.

In classic psychoanalysis, it is not unusual for a client to apply for treatment and then be selected if he or she is deemed an appropriate patient. Unsuitable candidates are not accepted. This guarantees that the analysis will have a high likelihood of success. But more important, the client selection process symbolizes the point that we are trying to make. Each therapy works best with a certain type of client or client problem. Psychoanalysis is to be applauded for recognizing that this treatment is not for everyone. Significant problems can occur when S4 methods are applied to clients who are at lower levels of task readiness. To use an S4 approach with populations such as psychopathic prisoners, low-functioning schizophrenics, or clients lacking behavioral skills is counterindicated by the ACT model.

The behavior of the analyst is consistent with the S4 conceptual framework. The therapist engages in minimal directive behavior and minimal supportive behavior. Too much relationship on the therapist's part will inhibit the critical transference process. Transference permits the patient to project onto the blank screen of the analyst manifestations of unresolved psychic conflicts. The analyst raises questions and calls attention to the cloudy or unfocused parts of the projected picture. In working through the transference, patients come to see themselves and the world with less distortion from unconscious conflicts.

The goal of psychoanalytic treatment is self-awareness and psychic conflict resolution rather than specific behavioral change. If these goals are met, then, perhaps, behavioral change will follow. The analysand does not need much relationship with the therapist because the essence of psychoanalysis is to "know thyself" (Arlow, 1977). With self-understanding as the goal and transference as a key therapeutic process, certain limits on the support dimension are thus established. As for the directive dimension, the patient's thoughts and associations are internally determined and should not be responses to external manipulation. This being the case, psychoanalysis provides little direction.

Many practitioners who espouse and use psychoanalytic theory do not limit their therapeutic style to the S4 quadrant. For example, some psychodynamically oriented clinicians use psychodrama, a therapy in which the therapist may use evocative, directive, active techniques to "turn the heat up" under a suspected repressed conflict. Much of the work of the post-Freudian psychoanalytic therapists has been directed toward the goal of accomplishing treatment more efficiently. In that process they have ventured out of S4 into more directive and more supportive styles. A Menninger-trained psychiatrist friend of ours described how, early in his career, he had made a very direct therapeutic suggestion to a certain client. The client, new to the city, was having trouble making friends and was lonely and unhappy. The psychiatrist could have stayed true to the analytic view which holds that if the client is lonely and unhappy, it reflects a psychic or interpersonal problem. Instead he chose to view the client's problem as not knowing how to go about meeting people and therefore suggested that the client volunteer to work for a local political candidate in order to increase the possibility of meeting interesting people. Having committed the heresy of being so directive, the fledgling psychiatrist reported nervously eyeing the picture of Dr. Karl Menninger which hung above his desk. After the client reported that the suggestion produced an excellent result, the psychiatrist began experimenting with a variety of treatment approaches without his initial feelings of disloyalty and trepidation. Despite his psychoanalytic training and continued psychodynamic conceptualization of cases, he is now quite well respected for developing and applying a number of innovative treatment plans.

A strict Freudian psychodynamic treatment plan has very limited application according to ACT. But the conceptualization of a problem and its treatment are two different things. A psychodynamic understanding of human behavior is certainly part of the conceptual repertoire of most practicing therapists. ACT recommends that practitioners use the full range of their life experience, education, and clinical experience to help them understand their clients. When it comes to actually deciding how to intervene effectively and therapeutically for clients, however, one needs to examine the key elements of client readiness according to ACT: motivation, ability, and confidence level. In all probability, an effective S4 approach to treatment will only apply to a small number of clinical situations.

Client-Centered Therapy: A Style 3 Approach

Symbolically and sometimes literally, the move from an S4 to an S3 therapeutic position brings the therapist's chair out from behind the couch. The client (never a patient) is face-to-face with a therapist who seeks to create the therapeutic conditions of acceptance, support, unconditional positive regard, and empathic understanding of that client's internal frame of reference. Client-centered therapy (Rogers, 1951) assumes that the client knows best and the therapist is present as a friendly helper in the client's own process. When exposed to the therapeutic conditions just cited, clients are able to explore, integrate, and accept themselves—to become autonomous, self-actualized persons who function effectively. The therapeutic relationship is both necessary and sufficient for change.

All approaches to therapy, except for a rare few instances in S1, focus some amount of attention on the therapeutic relationship. The variation among them concerns how much relationship is desirable and whether relationship alone is sufficient to produce change. ACT would predict the S3 style to be a good match and sufficient to produce change with clients who are reasonably willing and able to work on therapeutic tasks. C. H. Patterson, a client-centered therapy proponent, maintains his theoretical purity by claiming that lack of ability is an educational issue whereas lack of motivation is a therapeutic issue. By separating the two, therapy is only involved with the relationship or support dimension in our model.

> What about client problems that involve lack of information or knowledge, or lack of skills of various kinds? . . . Surely where these are lacking or inadequate the providing of a relationship is not sufficient. Although it might appear to be a resort to specious reasoning, dealing with such problems would appear to be education (or reeducation) or teaching rather than therapy. While it may be difficult to draw a line between therapy and (remedial) teaching there would seem to be some value in doing so. One difference might be that therapy is concerned with persons who are not lacking in knowledge or skills but who are unable for some reason to use their knowledge or skills. Their problem . . . is not one of learning but of performance. Therapy as a relationship is sufficient for enabling them to do those things that they are capable of doing. On the other hand the relationship may not be sufficient where there is a lack or deficit. It is here that the cognitive methods and techniques developed by Meichenbaum, for example, would be relevant and appropriate [Patterson, 1980, pp. 661–662].

Pure client-centered therapy does not even include a task dimension! For this reason, the selection of clients appropriate for this intervention style is just as critical as the selection of analysands for analysis. To be an effective form of treatment, client-centered therapy must be directed toward people who have prerequisite abilities. We wonder what a pure client-centered therapist would do with someone who honestly did not know how to do something. Such conjecturing reminds us of a young practicum student whose early supervision tapes were exemplary masterpieces of joining the client, establishing a therapeutic alliance, and helping the client to build self-esteem. The problem was that while the young counselor's empathy and clarification skills worked beautifully in the first few weeks of counseling, it became incredibly tiresome after seven or eight sessions to hear, "So what you're saying is . . . " At times, his clients would almost beg for direction, but the therapist was staunch in not violating the common dictum that we should not impose our values or advice on our clients.

We are also reminded of a woman who approached one of us after a day of consultation and announced that she was relieved to discover that there were practicing therapists who offered practical suggestions. She then proceeded to describe a fiasco she had personally experienced about six years earlier. She had sought treatment at that time while in the process of a divorce. The divorce was a real crisis in her life. In fact, she described herself as a basket case—as someone who could barely function. She felt that she was falling apart and needed someone to help her get her life in order. Instead, she claims she found herself face to face with a counselor whose only behavior consisted of listening, saying "uh-huh," and responding to the client's questions with "what do *you* think?" We suggest that this behavior is not always in the client's best interest. Carkhuff and Berenson (1967, p. 54) take a similar position when they observe that "we have built up a body of dogma in the psychoanalytic and client-centered approaches which appears to respond, in large part, to the need of the therapists rather than to the various levels of clients to whom they might attend."

Carl Rogers ran into the problem of how to provide the necessary direction when he attempted to extend his nondirective, client-centered techniques to psychologically disturbed clients. Rogers discovered that it was necessary to be much more verbally active in such a therapy process. In describing research applying person-centered therapy to a schizophrenic population, Meador and Rogers (1979) write about an interaction with a schizophrenic client. They describe the client as not seeming to find much meaning in the therapeutic relationship. Since the primary task of client-centered therapy is relationship building, Rogers was forced to do something else or give up when the relationship had no meaning or impact. It seems that whenever proponents of a particular approach to therapy have ventured outside of the client readiness range on which their approach was developed, they have had to change their style in a direction predicted by the ACT model. More often than not, strict proponents of a particular therapeutic stance work only with clients for whom the therapy is most likely to be effective.

Adlerian and Reality Therapy: Style 2 Approaches

As we shift our attention to S2 therapy, the range of therapeutic behavior continues to expand. Therapists using an S2 approach are high in direction and high in support. Adlerian and reality therapy, two S2 therapeutic approaches, involve much more active direction and structuring of therapeutic goals and processes by the therapist than either S4 or S3 modalities. While maintaining the relationship connection of S3, an S2 therapist is willing to be not only more directive but also more judgmental. Harold Mosak (1979), a proponent of Adlerian therapy, characterizes the therapist's behavior as "authentically himself—a caring, sharing person; who remains free to have feelings, opinions and to express them; revealing of himself as a person; task oriented; operating from a value base which is used in setting goals and evaluating behavior" (pp. 79–80). Both high-direction and high-support elements are prominent.

The Adlerian assumption of an active, directive role in therapy stems from the willingness of Adler and his proponents to leave the consulting room and venture into the community. The world outside the therapy office exposed Adler to a wider range of people who demonstrated great variability in readiness. Based on his experience, Adler could not conceive of the therapy process as being limited to a one-to-one, I–thou relationship within narrow confines. He believed in social action (child-care centers and public access to treatment), education (parenting skills and school consultation), and group and family therapy. (Adlerians were among the first to involve the families of a patient in treatment, recognizing that the person needing treatment, particularly a child, may be carrying the symptoms for someone else in the family or for the family system itself.) These global notions of therapy were his attempts to make treatment relevant for everyone, not just the elite.

Adlerians are quite willing to assume an S2 stance when necessary. They outline ways to convert the reluctant client into a willing one (Mosak and Shulman, 1963). Progress toward the goals of gaining insight into the "basic mistakes" that have led to a faulty life-style and reorienting toward a life-style of realistic expectations and positive social values can only be accomplished if the client is willing. The therapist's task is to convert the initially unwilling, but needing, client into a willing one.

William Glasser acknowledges the incorporation of Adlerian concepts into his reality therapy. Reality therapy (Glasser, 1965) is a clear example of a theory that developed out of the therapeutic needs of the originating population. The Ventura (California) School for Girls, whose residents were seriously delinquent adolescent girls, was the setting in which reality therapy principles developed. In ACT terms, residents were either unwilling, unable, lacking in confidence, or some combination of the three. Appropriate intervention would thus consist of high-direction/low-support or high-direction/high-support therapist behavior. Reality therapy concepts, such as the importance of identity, positive self-concept, and individual autonomy, are directly related to ACT concepts of task-relevant readiness levels and the therapist styles appropriate to them. Glasser and Zunin (1979, p. 314) describe the abilities that reality therapy can instill in its clients if it is successful: "This is the ability to let go and relinquish environmental supports and substitute internal psychological support, the ability of an individual to psychologically stand on his own two feet. This, of course, does not mean not to be involved, not to give, not to love, and so forth. It means for the individual to take responsibility for who he is and what he wants in life and to develop responsible plans to fulfill his needs and his goals."

At this point we turn to an illustration to show how certain readiness levels naturally require differential therapist responses. If the client says, "If you want me to do this, I'll do it for you," a Rogerian or S3 therapist might respond, "If you want to do it, don't do it for me, do it for yourself." Glasser, in working with R1 and R2 clients, found that "to ask people to make commitments for themselves is often too much to ask. Therefore if the client says to a reality therapist, 'I'll do it for you,' the reality therapist, in the early and intermediate stage of therapy, will respond favorably and positively" (Glasser and Zunin, 1979, p. 322).

Reality therapy sessions are goal-specific and structured. Reality therapy represents the heavy use of style 2 coupled with use of style 1 as necessary. A reality therapist focuses frequently on pinning down the client. This pinning down can be clearly seen in the planning of behavioral goals. If a teen-age girl who has never sought a job before says to a reality therapist, "Next week I am going to look for my first job," the therapist would not say, "Good, let me know how it works out." The reality therapist is more likely to respond with a series of very precise questions such as Glasser (1965, pp. 324–325) describes:

Therapist	What day next week?
Girl:	I don't know. I thought Monday or Tuesday.
Therapist:	Which day, Monday or Tuesday?
Girl:	Well, I guess Tuesday.
Therapist:	You guess or will it be Tuesday?
Girl:	Tuesday
Therapist:	What time Tuesday?
Girl:	Well, sometime in the morning.
Therapist:	What time in the morning?
Girl:	Oh, well, nine thirty.
Therapist:	Fine, that is a good time to begin looking for a job. What do you plan to wear?
Girl:	Well, I never thought it would make a difference. What do you think I should wear?
Therapist:	(*Discuss several alternatives to grooming and dress relative to job hunting*). How are you going to look up what jobs to apply for ?
Girl:	I thought I would look in the morning paper in the classified section.

> *Therapist:*   (*The therapist might discuss the pros and cons*
> *of also looking in the Sunday paper as the girl*
> *may not be aware of the larger classified sec-*
> *tion on that day of the week. The therapist*
> *might even go through the classified section*
> *with her.*)

This example shows the therapist shifting to S2 in order to ensure that all the directive questions of who, what, when, where, and how are answered. Instruction is offered when the client lacks information or competence. At this point in the therapy process, a positive relationship has already been established and serves as a cushion for this pinning-down process.

The label for S2 therapies is *teach*. The S2 therapist is comfortable teaching the willing, but unable, client alternative ways of looking at the world and relating to it. From this perspective, it is consistent to view psychotherapy as "a cooperative educational enterprise . . . with the . . . subject matter of this course in re-education being the patient himself—his lifestyle and his relationship to the life tasks" (Mosak, 1979, p. 64).

Adlerian and reality therapy include learning and teaching as integral elements in effecting behavioral change. The developmental "match and move" principles of ACT are evident, especially in reality therapy. Match the client where he is and move toward R4 functioning as the client finds himself having attained identity, responsibility, and commitment.

Just as there is a client population for whom S4 or S3 therapies would be inappropriate, so too there are client populations for whom S2 approaches to counseling would not be treatments of choice. Imagine counseling the recently retired CEO of a large corporation, a man who has been successful in all the major areas of his life. He is seeking therapy now as he struggles with some of his concerns and feelings related to retirement. To pin him down as Glasser does the young girl in the preceding example would be belittling. We have every reason to believe that this man will be able to redirect his energies once he has worked through his feelings. An S2 approach is far too directive. For the time being at least, the most he needs is an understanding ear and someone to help him clarify his confusion.

Behaviorism and RET: Style 1 Approaches

Two therapeutic approaches associated with high-directive and low-supportive therapist styles are operant behavior therapy, developed by B. F. Skinner, and rational-emotive therapy (RET), developed by Albert Ellis. Style 1 therapists seem to say, in effect, "Give me control over a relevant array of reinforcers and I can evoke behavior change in clients. We may not even need to like each other."

Style 1 involves the use of directive therapist behavior, external rewards and punishments, and low emotional affect from the therapist. In order for S1 to be the dominant style, significant external motivation and reinforcers are necessary. Whether pellets from a Skinner box, pieces of candy in toilet training, or points in a token economy, the use of rewards and sanctions, which are external but relevant to the client, are necessary to shift behavior in the desired direction. Style 1 interventions are unemotional straightforward emphases on task. An S1 interventionist would say, "I'm not angry at you or punishing you. I do, however, expect you to make your bed before you will be served breakfast. Making your bed is a part of your responsibilities as a member of this group. Here's how to make the bed."

Behavioral approaches have been extremely helpful in institutional settings, where the residents may be unwilling or unable to take care of themselves. The ACT model would predict that unless new behavior is internalized (which means, in effect, that the client has progressed in terms of readiness), the new behavior will stop as soon as the controls on the contingencies are removed. It is this lack of development with respect to readiness that explains why our prisons and substance abuse programs function as revolving doors. The client may stay clean or dry while access to a weapon or drug is externally controlled, but as soon as the environmental controls are lifted, the old problematic behavior returns. To be truly successful, treatment must include a process by which the client becomes less externally and more internally motivated. Effective treatment, as we will show later, requires that the therapist move with the client through various stages and styles as the client's readiness develops. An example of S1 treatment occurs thousands of times daily in America as overweight people participate in commercial weight-loss programs that involve very strict and very structured diets. The foods for each meal are prescribed and sometimes even prepackaged. Successful dieters may even be refunded part of the money for a particular program to increase their motivation. These programs have great value in helping dieters control their eating behavior. However, dieters who participate in these commercial weight-loss programs often leap from this S1 treatment program into an S4 situation as soon as they reach their desired weight. Once the programmatic structure is removed, they are on their own. The new weight becomes difficult to maintain because new eating habits have not yet been internalized. In contrast, well-conceived behavioral approaches to weight control assist clients in translating new learning about eating into their everyday living.

Ellis (1979) refers to less directive and more supportive therapy styles as "indulgence therapy" (p. 295) and says they are much less efficient than the "highly cognitive, active-directive, homework-assigning and discipline-oriented therapies like RET" (p. 86). He employs a rapid-fire, active, directive, persuasive methodology in working through a client's faulty cognitions or irrational beliefs. The goal is for clients eventually to adopt a rational-emotive cognitive set by which to interpret their internal and external world. ACT would predict the presence of considerable supportive behavior from the RET therapist as the client proceeds to adopt a more rational belief system. Psychoanalytic writers see Ellis in their own terms as mitigating the influence of the superego by giving the client a new superego. Psychodynamically inclined thinkers such as Jacob Arlow compare what Ellis does to religious conversion. Arlow says, "Some preach the 10 commandments, Ellis preaches the 11 irrational Beliefs. . . . The priest says 'Stop masturbating.' Ellis says 'Stop musturbating'" (Arlow, 1977, p. 4).

It is possible to incorporate Ellis's ideas and use a broader style of therapy than just S1. The ACT model would contend that Ellis's S1 approach would match R1 clients by bolstering their confidence through skill development and providing a specific, structured framework. Once the confidence and skill level improve, motivation too is likely to increase. Then the RET therapist can engage in increasingly supportive and less directive behavior. ACT would also contend that clients at higher developmental levels of task readiness would not remain long with an S1 therapist. People who can control their own behavior do not generally enjoy being controlled. Style 1 therapy is, in fact, best used with persons who have never developed, or have temporarily lost, control over the behavior around which they are in therapeutic need. Crisis situations, in particular, require S1 behavior from the intervenor. The divorced woman described earlier in the chapter who said she was a "basket case" was disgruntled with her counselor's S3 approach precisely because her crisis state was screaming for some external controls. Such controls as security guards, isolation rooms, and time-outs are S1 responses for out-of-control residents or inmates in institutional settings.

Applying ACT to Other Therapies

There are several other therapeutic approaches that bear discussion. Gestalt therapy (Perls, 1969) can be placed in the S4 quadrant even though it is somewhat more directive than psychoanalysis. (We hope it is clear by now that no quadrant has a static point of directiveness and supportiveness.) In Gestalt therapy the therapeutic task is to have the person confront and integrate internal conflict. While the method is similar to the blank screen of psychoanalysis, the therapist uses somewhat directive behavior. The empty chair technique is a classic example of Gestalt. Once the client identifies his internal dilemma, he is instructed in the process of moving back and forth between the positions that symbolize his internal conflict. But, he executes the process in his own way and under his own direction.

The humanistic approach to psychotherapy is rooted in the person-centered assumptions of Rogers (1961) and in the self-actualizing ideas of Maslow (1954). Actualizing therapies assume that problems are a matter of lack of confidence or thwarted motivation. There is almost no focus on skill development. Most humanists use an S3 and S4 set of therapist styles. There is a varying amount of support and little direction. A look at experiments with humanistic education provides telling evidence to support the importance of assessing a client's readiness level before applying a particular theoretical stance. In humanistic educational settings, teachers give support while students engage in self-directed learning. This style has been enormously successful with bright, motivated, and skilled students. Humanistic education failed, however, when it was applied to less able, less motivated students. In fact, even if a student was highly motivated but lacked essential academic skills, humanistic education failed. One of the authors watched with pride as her daughter flowered and grew at a nontraditional, humanistically based college. She also watched with dismay as other students—students who were not selected on the appropriate criteria—floundered and flailed and never completed their educations.

Family therapy is a school of therapy comprising many approaches. The unifying thread is the belief that it is important to work with the entire family system for successful therapeutic change. How therapy is conducted, however, draws on the full range of ACT criteria. Every therapy situation involves 100 percent support and 100 percent direction. It is simply a matter of who supplies what part of each. While, in general, family therapists rely on high-direction strategies (S1 and S2), the various schools of family therapy fall within all of the quadrants. Since the application of ACT to family therapy warrants a book of its own, most of the cases reviewed in this book are individual cases. Once the reader has a thorough working knowledge of ACT, however, its application to other therapy situations should become obvious.

The Value of Having Four Treatment Styles

It stands to reason that if various therapies developed because they worked best with a particular client population, then therapists who maintain a varied caseload will be most effective if they employ an eclectic approach. Benefits result from applying different therapeutic approaches to different clients. If therapists using only one theory or one set of techniques do not limit their practice to only one kind of client, treatment problems will ensue.

The principles of ACT seem to have been embedded in the theory and practice of all effective therapists, whatever their theoretical persuasion. The research of Fred Fiedler (1950, 1951) has demonstrated that experienced therapists behave in much more similar ways than their theoretical affiliation or self-report of their behavior would have predicted. It is our contention that such therapists have in common an intuitive understanding of the ACT model, the adherence to which makes them more like than unlike one another. In working with clients, one tends to do whatever will work, and good therapists from all persuasions tend to do similar things when confronted with similar client problems. A slightly different, but related, point can be made if one looks at the review of the research on therapeutic outcomes by Smith, Glass, and Miller (1980). This review indicates that despite the differences in therapists' techniques, different psychotherapies are equally effective. We would suggest that effectiveness is the result of the appropriate matching of client readiness and therapist style. That different psychotherapies are equally effective is consistent with the ACT model as long as each therapy is used with clients from the appropriate range of readiness levels.

In this chapter, we have examined several major theoretical approaches to psychotherapy from the ACT perspective. We believe that while some clinical problems can be handled with a single approach to therapy, other situations dictate the use of two or more styles of therapy because of the complexity of the therapeutic issues and because clients vary in readiness for their different therapeutic goals. We will present clinical illustrations of situations involving different configurations of therapist styles after we have discussed how to apply ACT to treatment planning. But first Chapter Four will give you the opportunity to examine your own stylistic range and preferences.

4

How to Assess Your Therapeutic Style and Adaptability

At the end of Chapter One, we asked you to complete the Therapist Style Inventory (TSI). In the present chapter we describe the structure of the TSI measure, explain its relationship to ACT theory, demonstrate how to obtain three scale scores from this instrument, and consider some therapist profiles that emerge from it.

Therapist Style Preference

As explained earlier, the core of ACT theory lies in its value for matching a therapist's style of intervention to the therapeutic task readiness of the client. The twelve situations described in TSI depict three instances for each of the four levels of client readiness. The four therapist reactions to each situation, from which you were asked to choose, represent responses from each of the four possible therapist styles. If you were to choose the therapist style response suggested by ACT theory to each of the twelve situations, you would have chosen three responses from each style. The first scale score that the TSI provides is called therapist style preference. A therapist who indicated three responses from each style category would show no obvious preference for a particular therapist style and thus would be categorized as having preferred styles 1 through 4. At the other extreme, someone else might have selected the same therapist style in all twelve situations—for example, all S1 or "telling" responses. Such a person would obviously have a clear style preference. You can score your TSI for style preference by using the form presented in Table 2.

Table 2. Key for Scoring Therapist Style on the TSI and Style Range Scales.

Situation	Therapist Style Range: Intervention Style Choice			
	Style 1	Style 2	Style 3	Style 4
1	A	B	C	D
2	A	B	D	C
3	A	B	C	D
4	C	A	B	D
5	A	B	C	D
6	D	A	B	C
7	A	C	B	D
8	A	B	C	D
9	A	D	C	B
10	D	B	A	C
11	A	D	C	B
12	B	C	D	A
Total:	_____	_____	_____	_____
	Tell	Teach	Support	Delegate

(Add number
of circled items
for each column)

Enter the data from your TSI responses in Table 2 in the following manner:

1. Find your answer to situation 1 on the TSI form.
2. Circle the letter response you chose (A, B, C, D) in the horizontal row marked situation 1.
3. Repeat the same procedure until your responses to all twelve situations are entered in Table 2.
4. Count the number of circled items in the column labeled style 1, and enter that number in the row labeled Total of that column.
5. Repeat the same procedure for the remaining three columns, entering in the appropriate number of circles for each column in the row labeled Total.

By considering the numbers in the row marked Total, you can derive a sense of your style preference. The column with the largest number of chosen responses represents your basic therapeutic style preference. Three responses from each of the four columns suggest total style flexibility (or no particular style preference). A therapist who has 6 points in style 2 and 6 points in style 3 is a therapist who focuses on high relationship but is flexible with regard to the amount of direction he or she uses. All points in style 1 and style 2 would suggest a therapist's pattern of preferring high-direction therapies. Seven or more responses in any one style indicate that the therapist prefers one style over all others.

A therapist's supporting style is any style category, other than the preferred style, which has a score of 2 or more. (This scoring is in keeping with Hersey and Blanchard's 1977 concept related to leadership style.) Supporting styles are those one tends to use on occasion. Fewer than two responses in any style category indicates that a therapist is unlikely to use that style. Table 3 presents a pattern of response to the TSI and shows how each pattern might be characterized regarding both preferred and supporting styles. A therapist obviously could have from one to four preferred styles and from zero to three supporting styles.

Therapist Style Range

Another name for style range is style flexibility. The therapist's style range refers to the number of styles a therapist has at his or her command. Style range information can be obtained by examining the Total row of Table 2. If a therapist has two or more responses in any style category, that therapist has access to that style. Turning to Table 3, you can see that the hypothetical therapist named Bob would have a style range of 4; Mary has a style range of 1; Tim's style range score is 2; and Jane possesses a style range score of 2.

While it is generally true that a greater style range is preferred, this statement must be interpreted with extreme caution. Although our fictitious therapist named Bob has a style range of 4, it is still possible that he does not match his style

Table 3. Patterns of Response to the TSI and
Corresponding Characterizations for Hypothetical Individuals.

		Number of Responses			
Therapist	Style 1	Style 2	Style 3	Style 4	Characterization
Bob	3	3	3	3	Basic style 1, 2, 3, 4
Mary	0	10	1	1	Basic style 2, no supporting style
Tim	6	6	0	0	Basic styles 1 and 2, no supporting style
Jane	2	7	3	0	Basic style 2, supporting styles 1 and 3

to the readiness level of his clients. Likewise, Mary has a style range of 1, which at first blush looks distressing. Yet, if this style matched the readiness level of her clients, her total use of S2 interventions would be indicated by our model. Hence, knowledge of style preference and style flexibility cannot fully predict therapeutic efficacy. However, the preceding caveats lead to consideration of the match between client task-relevant readiness and therapist style. The TSI scale that addresses this central issue is the therapist adaptability scale.

Therapist Adaptability

The therapist adaptability or therapist effectiveness score represents the degree to which a therapist chooses the style of therapeutic response predicted to be optimal for the client's readiness. You can obtain your effectiveness score by entering the data from your TSI scale responses in Table 4.

Scoring for therapist adaptability begins by noting the letter of the response you chose for situation 1 and circling the number found under that letter along the row designated for situation 1. For example, if you chose response D to situation 1, you would circle the value "1" in that top row. If you selected response A for situation 2, you would circle the value "3" in the second row of numbers. Enter the data on your responses to the twelve situations in this manner. Then sum the circled values for each column and enter that sum in the row labeled

Table 4. Key for Scoring Therapist Adaptability Scale of the TSI.

Situation	Intervention Choice			
	A	B	C	D
1	4	3	2	1
2	3	4	1	2
3	1	3	4	2
4	2	3	1	4
5	4	3	2	1
6	4	3	2	1
7	1	4	2	3
8	1	2	3	4
9	4	1	2	3
10	2	4	1	3
11	1	2	4	3
12	4	1	2	3
Subtotal:	____ +	____ +	____ +	____ = Total

Subtotal in that column. These four subtotals are then summed to yield your total therapist adaptability score.

Several points should be made regarding the therapist adaptability score, which can range from 12 to 48. A score of 48 means that the therapist chose the style predicted to be optimally effective by ACT theory on each of the twelve items. On the other hand, a score close to 12 indicates a poor match between therapist style and the demands of the clinical situation. In other words, the best choices of therapist style receive a value of 4 in Table 4, while the poorer choices receive values of 1, 2, or 3, depending upon the degree of mismatch. Assigning one of these three values to an incorrect response follows the general relationship outlined in Table 1. Note that in Table 1 the choice of supporting (S3) and teaching (S2) therapist styles (styles that include high relationship behaviors) are never designated as having the lowest probability of success. This fact implies that one might consider choosing a high relationship response when one is totally unsure of the client's readiness. It is never entirely wrong to be a supportive human being.

Because the TSI is based upon situations in which clients demonstrated a broad range of readiness levels, it was necessary to employ a broad range of therapist styles to obtain a high therapist adaptability score. Does this imply that a therapist who uses a limited range of styles is bound to be ineffective according to the ACT model? The answer is no. If a therapist limits his or her practice to clients with a limited range of readiness levels and then delivers the style of interventions appropriate to those clients, ACT predicts success for those contacts in spite of the narrow range of styles. In fact, if a therapist sees clients in a narrow band of readiness levels but employs a broad range of therapist styles, by definition some of the choices of style would represent mismatches.

To illustrate the relationship of style range to therapeutic effectiveness, it may help to discuss several clinical situations in which a counselor works full-time with a particular set of problems. Therapists, for example, who work in a clinic dealing with problem pregnancies and whose job it is to help people make the significant decisions related to unwanted pregnancy can be most effective at their jobs if they generally limit their behavior to an S2 style. Successful counseling in this delicate area generally requires supportive behavior and a therapeutic process that helps clients sort out their own situation and their own feelings. Some direction would be necessary for the client. The counselor might need to educate the client about the range of available options, and once a choice is made the client might well need help in implementing the decision. By the same token, most of us would be appalled by a counselor in this situation who told the client, "You should get an abortion," or "You should keep the child," or "You need to make arrangements for adoption." The S1 style would be inappropriate. It would also be problematic if a counselor offered no support to these clients or provided no direction whatsoever. It would be difficult for a client to make a decision about a pregnancy problem without any knowledge of the range of options. By not offering support or direction, a counselor would be operating from a strict S4 stance—also inappropriate. Keep in mind that directive and supportive behaviors are not discrete. Although we have divided these behaviors into the four quadrants, they fall on a continuum. If we had to select the ideal stance for the pregnancy counselor, it would be in the center of the upper part of the S2 quadrant—high support and some direction, as illustrated in Figure 3. A counselor who operated anywhere close to the ideal stance would probably be successful.

Figure 3. The Pregnancy Counselor's Style.

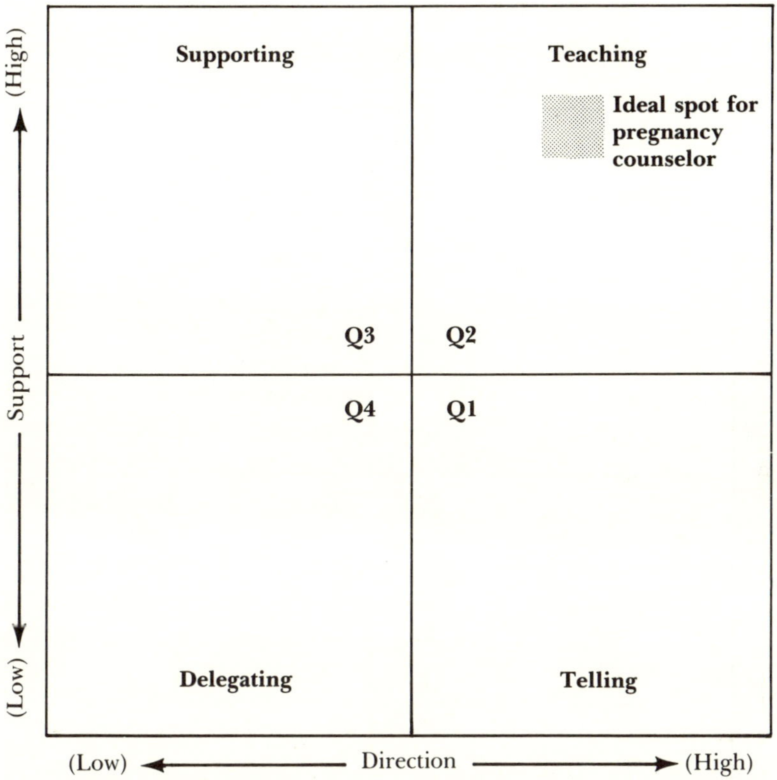

To continue with this illustration, imagine the counselor whose job it is to counsel the rebellious and lawbreaking adolescent entering a court-mandated drug treatment program. Catastrophe would be the result for a counselor who possessed only S3 or S4 skills. These young people need direction. While support can be helpful, direction is mandatory. To be understood and supported is one thing. To change behavior that is highly problematic is another. ACT would predict that counselors who could only hold hands, understand, and empathize would fail with these young people, while counselors who could provide direction and some support would succeed. Ideally such a counselor would work primarily with an S1 or an S2 style as long as he or she employed directive behavior and used some supportive behavior as shown in Figure 4.

Figure 4. The Adolescent Counselor's Style.

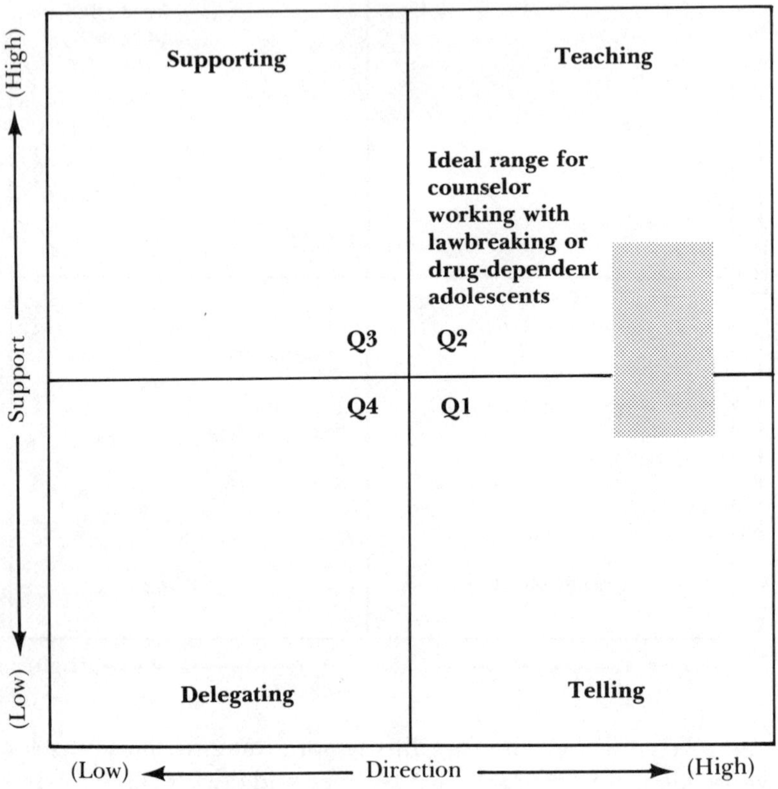

The interpretation of the therapist adaptability score, therapist preferred style scores, and therapist range scores is not immediately obvious. You can obtain useful information by considering each item on the TSI individually, noting your choice of therapy style for situations depicting different levels of client readiness.

Preferred Style Interpretations

We can translate the various patterns of preferred and supporting styles into typical personalities. Each example presents the professional issues that are likely to arise. We will be identifying various well-known personalities such as therapists, politicians, and sports figures with prominent styles. You are encouraged to think about other famous people you know in terms of these styles.

Preferred Style 1: Tell. Persons with a preferred orientation of style 1 tend to be very task-oriented, like to set clear goals, and work toward these goals. Such people have definite ideas about how things should be done, and they are willing to direct others along those paths. Style 1 people tend to overlook emotional nuances in the pursuit of task accomplishment.

Famous Style 1 Individuals. The prototypical style 1 psychotherapist is Albert Ellis. A frequent comment by many people attending Ellis's presentations can be paraphrased as "I didn't much care for him, but I think his ideas are valuable." We think Ellis would respond by saying that it is important that people learn to live rationally but not important that they like him. Certainly, we agree that therapy can be considered successful when clients change for the better. Many of the early behavioral orientations discounted the importance of relationship behavior and pressed for clear behavioral goals and methods of treatment. Ellis's approach works well with people who are in sufficient pain to want relief. Relief rather than relationship is what they crave. Ellis also is a well-known and well-respected expert and can therefore get away with less relationship behavior than most of the rest of us. We would predict that his style would not work well in situations where the client feels competent to make changes but does not know what changes to make. Likewise there is a difference between the client who feels guilty because he obsessively talks irrationally to himself and the client who has been ashamed of some behavior and has been carrying that shame around. The first client's guilt would be helped by the

S1 approach of Ellis. The second client's guilt would more likely be helped by cathartic sharing and by an S3 therapist who could listen and understand the client's shame.

In sports, Woody Hayes is style 1 all the way! Coach Hayes ended his career by punching an opposing player . . . all direction and zero support by anyone's definition. Hayes's brand of football was the "grind it out" version. For years, he was successful with his "three yards in a cloud of dust" approach. Hayes wasted considerable talent, however, as reflected by professional players like Paul Warfield and others who were much more productive as professionals than they were in college. This was because Hayes made players fit his system. The system did not adjust to the unique talents of individual players.

As for political military figures, General George Patton ran a disciplined army, but he lacked the ability to engage in relationship behavior. ACT would predict that Patton's S1 leadership style would work best with an army that was in the early phases of organization, was under the crisis conditions of war (the situation within which he did indeed flourish), or had been organized at one time but was now falling down on the job. Competent and experienced peers, even officers of a lower rank, would no doubt struggle with Patton's style. Because he lacked relationship skills, Patton had to influence peers and superiors by employing the power of his office. (The importance of power in this model is discussed in Chapter Seven.)

As with any style, the degree of effectiveness depends on the client's readiness level and the direction in which performance is moving. Style 1 therapists tend to be effective in crisis situations where followers are looking for strong direction. They also tend to succeed when they have predominant power in a situation. And they are good at getting the attention of unwilling clients. When the power is not there, when the crisis is not resolved, or when the client is willing and able to choose from a variety of positive options, the S1 therapist is lacking the necessary range of skills.

Preferred Style 2: Teach. Therapists who prefer style 2 tend to enjoy working with others to accomplish tasks. They are comfortable being in charge, but they want motivated clients who value and accept the goals of therapy. Style 2 therapists enjoy the teaching and the developmental process. They hope to transfer knowledge and skills to their clients. Such therapists generally like their young birds to leave the nest after learning. Style 2 therapists tend to sell their goals and methods.

Famous Style 2 Individuals. Alfred Adler and Sigmund Freud exemplify style 2 in terms of their roles as trainers of other therapists. Both were excellent at attracting and training persons who wanted to learn about their systems of therapy. Adler let his trainee birds out of the nest when he sensed they were ready to fly on their own. Freud, however, seemed to have trouble accepting his fledglings as colleagues and equals. As a therapist, too, Adler operated with a primarily S2 style. His therapy, as noted in an earlier chapter, provided a lot of direction while also being supportive. Freud's psychoanalytic therapy was, of course, an S4 therapy style. Most readers can probably remember a significant teacher who was very influential in their early professional development. Since S2 is a style that involves mostly teaching, it is likely that most of your professional role models used a number of S2 behaviors.

Many of the significant coaching figures in college sports operate from an S2 stance. Paul "Bear" Bryant and George Thompson demonstrate concern not only for performance, but for the individual student-athlete as well. Style 2 coaches receive a great deal of loyalty and affection from their players. As coaches they excel at developing their players' skill and improving their performance. Vince Lombardi and other professional coaches like him are master communicators who use the S2 approach with their players.

In politics, Franklin Roosevelt, John Kennedy, and Ronald Reagan represent presidents with an S2 approach. While S2 has a "teach" label in the ACT model, it carries a "sell" label in leadership theory. Using a preferred S2 approach, augmented with a supporting style, both Reagan and Roosevelt were able to push through pet programs despite significant opposition. Kennedy's use of style 2 can be observed in the way he sold the nation on the space program and the need to pursue civil rights issues. Roosevelt, Kennedy, and Reagan represent a considerable range of political thought and have sold very different goals. The content in each administration has been different, but the style and process are remarkably similar. Style 2 leaders are usually very well liked. Indicative of this is the fact that even Walter Mondale, Reagan's arch political adversary, has said he likes Reagan. Such unexpected plaudits are likely due to high relationship behavior on Reagan's part.

Preferred Style 3: Support. Style 3 is characterized by high levels of supportive relationship behavior. Style 3 therapists are very comfortable with active listening, empathic understanding and supportive behavior. They enjoy working with clients who are willing and able to set their own goals for therapy. Style 3 therapists are less comfortable behaving didactically. They generally do not like to ''teach'' or ''tell'' unless their supporting style is S1 or S2. Rather than pressing for clear, explicit goals, therapists who work primarily with an S3 approach are more likely to trust the therapy process and trust clients to do things in their own time and way. Although confrontation can be used as a form of support, primary S3 therapists may find confrontation and open conflict difficult.

Famous Style 3 Individuals. Carl Rogers represents the classic S3 therapist. It has been said of Rogers that if you met him somewhere by chance, you would leave convinced that he came there specifically to see you. Whether this is an accurate description of Rogers's impact on others or not, it is an accurate description of the effect on others of most S3 behavior. Rogers, who does an excellent job of providing client support, believes in clients' ability to direct their own therapy if they have the therapist's support.

In sports, more professional coaches appear to have a dominant S3 style than do college coaches. This pattern would be consistent with the ACT model. For the most part, the professional athlete is more willing and has more ability than the college athlete. All that may be needed from the coach is support in polishing skills and developing the team. Bob Lemon, the baseball manager, exemplifies S3 leadership in sports. In working with competent and motivated players, he knows how to stroke egos, ask for suggestions, and support and motivate his players.

In politics, President Jimmy Carter's natural style was S3. He campaigned and won by saying "I'm an honest, God-fearing man (not one of the Watergate-type politicians) and will respect the people and listen to what they have to say." The Camp David Agreement between Egypt and Israel was Carter's major success. As mediator for that agreement, Carter reflected the S3 pattern of listening for and reflecting elements common to both sides, supporting the negotiation process, but not forcing a solution. As president, Carter also reflected a deficit of S2 skills. He was unable to "sell" any of his major initiatives to Congress or to the public. An energy policy, human rights legislation, and the Olympic boycott were all defeated because he never was able to sell these goals to the public.

Preferred Style 4: Delegate. Few leaders, and probably few readers, prefer style 4. As you may recall, S4 individuals provide little support and little direction. Neither the characteristics needed for leadership nor the characteristics needed to be a helping professional would make S4 behavior come naturally to those engaged in such processes. This style is appropriate in leadership situations and in therapy when things are going well. At such times the S4 maxim—"If it isn't broken, don't fix it"—is entirely appropriate. Within an organization where people are productive, willing, and able, the best approach is to let people do what they are already doing. The S4 leader values noninterference and trusts the process or the people to work things out. The S4 leader is likely to avoid making decisions or giving directions. In so doing, he or she allows, encourages, or forces others into the directive position. The classic analytic S4 stance was rooted in the belief that observation of the unconscious processes as well as the transference was impeded by too much activity by the analyst. If you are always stirring the water with a stick, you just obscure the bottom.

Famous Style 4 Individuals. As previously mentioned, the behavior of the classic analyst is primarily S4. The S4 quadrant, however, like the other three, includes a range of behavior. Among analysts and other S4 therapists, a total lack of either support or direction would be difficult to imagine. Such a notion is counter to what we call therapeutic process. Many therapists, with other preferred styles, appropriately use S4 behaviors as termination approaches. Where previously they supported and reinforced the client for taking certain positive steps, for example, they now ask the client, ''How do you feel about that?'' In this way, they are slowly withdrawing their support from the client and helping him to internalize support for himself.

In sports, the very term *coaching* suggests that we are not likely to find any pure S4 leaders in the coaching business. Style 4 behavior is more likely to come from team owners, perhaps because the owners assume they have hired competent and motivated coaches. Style 4 owners are likely to say, ''You're the manager or coach, you run the team. I'll check the paper periodically to see how you're doing. Call if you need anything.'' Clint Murchison of the Dallas Cowboys and Guy Lewis of the Houston Cougars are good examples of this S4 approach. There is one classic sports example, involving the owner of a team, which reflects the importance of matching style to task readiness. George Steinbrenner, owner of the New York Yankees, set a goal of having the best baseball team his money could buy. With that goal in mind, he bought Reggie Jackson, Dave Winfield, and several others, all of them very competent and highly motivated baseball players. Unfortunately, Steinbrenner then hired Billy Martin, a preferred S1/S2 manager, to manage this group of high-priced egos and talent. Predictably such a combination did not produce positive results. Exit Billy Martin and enter Bob Lemon. Lemon, as we mentioned earlier, used an S3 management approach. It did not take long for the Yankees to move from fifth place to first place in their division and to win both the pennant and the World Series. But apparently Steinbrenner is slow to learn about style matches. He eventually fired Lemon.

In politics, Eisenhower was primarily an S4 president. He was leading a nation that was basking in the victory of World War II and prospering. We were a people who believed in our own competence and our own motivation. We felt we had the world by the tail. We loved watching Ike play golf; his leisure became a symbolic statement of the comfortable nature of things. Since the nation was running smoothly, a more active or supportive president was unnecessary. (By contrast, when President Reagan planned an extended vacation during a period of national unrest, his constituency was appalled. Reagan's followers needed their S2 leader to be available.) As general, prior to his presidency, Eisenhower's skills at building support and delegating (S3 and S4) were very well suited for coping with Montgomery, de Gaulle, Patton, and others, competent leaders who wanted to be left alone.

Supporting Style and Developing Style

The characteristics of the preferred style are modified by the pattern of supporting and developing styles. Your *supporting* style is a style in which you are strong but not as strong as in your preferred style. If you have a strong supporting style adjacent to your preferred style, it adds strength in that direction to the preferred style. An adjacent style in the ACT model is a style that is in the next quadrant to the therapist's preferred style. If you are an S4, then S3 is your adjacent style. If you are primarily an S2, you have two possible adjacent styles, S1 and S3. If your preferred style is S2 and S3 is your supporting style, then your preference would be in the direction of relationship therapies. On the other hand, if your preferred style is S2 and S1 is your supporting style, then your preference would be for directing therapies. High-relationship patterns are the most frequent patterns among therapists. High-relationship styles work well with the majority of self-referred, motivated clients or colleagues. Therapists who are low in S2 and S3 behavior may be too directive. This would be the case for a therapist whose preferred style is S1 and whose supporting style is S2. If a therapist's preferred style is S4 and S3 is his or her supporting style, there may be a tendency to let clients fend for themselves with respect to a task. Clearly, these patterns would not be problematic if the therapist's clients matched the therapist's style. High-relationship therapists tend to provide more support than is needed and fail to match that support to performance at the lower levels of willingness. High-directive therapists tend to err in not using support as a reinforcer for therapy tasks.

A *developing* style in the ACT model refers to styles of therapist behavior that do not come naturally to the therapist and must be focused on if they are to be learned and incorporated in the practitioner's repertoire for greater range and flexibility. A therapist's developing style is a style that he or she does not currently use well. For therapists most comfortable with directive therapies, goals for improving style flexibility and range might include developing the behavior associated with patience and working for client discovery rather than therapist interpretation and teaching. Low-directive therapists, by contrast, may wish to examine their therapeutic interactions and look for ways in which they might more effectively lead their clients. They might consider experimenting with being more direct with directions. Low-directive psychotherapists may be operating from a strong set of theoretical injunctions that place directive responses out of bounds.

Disjunctive Style Patterns

If the major support for a preferred style is not next door but at least a style category away, both therapist and client may have difficulty making progress in therapy. Thus, developing strength in the intermediate styles is indicated. To illustrate this point, we turn to a story one of our clients brought to therapy.

Marcia came to therapy because she was very indecisive— so much so that she felt as if she were not functioning appropriately. The therapist began by gathering some history about the client. (The therapy process, by the way, used mostly S2 therapist behavior. The therapist structured the questions sufficiently to keep them targeted to the presenting problem while engaging in relationship behavior that helped the client to relax about the therapy process.) Eventually, Marcia told the following story. Until she was thirteen years old, Marcia's mother purchased all of Marcia's clothes without consulting her daughter at all. Mother also carefully selected everything Marcia was to wear each day and laid all of the clothes out on Marcia's bed for her. This is an absolute S1 stance. The mother was saying, in effect, "I will decide what you are to wear and when you are to wear it. You cannot make any decisions about the matter of clothes." The only self-directed behavior permitted to Marcia with regard to clothing was that she was expected to dress herself. Suddenly, at age thirteen, Marcia was told that while she still could not select her own clothing purchases, she was now expected to get herself dressed each day with no help from her mother. Marcia then reported the following: "The first few days I would put on some kind of outfit only to come downstairs to my mother's angry criticism and disdain. Usually, she would instruct me to go back upstairs and try again. There were literally mornings that I would dress, come downstairs, and be sent back up again five or six times. In time, I became more and more anxious about which clothes to wear. I couldn't figure out what skirt went with what top and so forth. But I'm not hopelessly stupid, you know, so eventually I did figure out how things were supposed to go together in a tasteful fashion."

Marcia's mother was what we will call the "one-four flop." She began teaching Marcia how to dress herself in an S1 manner. She did all the directing of the process. This is not a bad place to begin with a very young child who knows nothing about dressing herself. Mother's very next move, unfortunately, was to the S4 position where she expected to delegate the entire process to Marcia. The ACT model claims that a successful learning process, whether it be therapeutic learning, learning from a parent, or learning in school, requires that the learner be taken through a process that begins at the learner's readiness level and ends with the learner fully ready to take over the task for him- or herself. A more effective parent would have followed the S1 stance by describing to Marcia *why* she was selecting the particular clothing items (S2). She might then ask Marcia to guess which tops might match a particular skirt (S2). Then mother might say, "Today you select your outfit and I'll tell you if there are problems with it" (S3). In time, more and more of the responsibility would be transferred from mother to Marcia. Marcia would thus be developing her ability and her confidence in dressing herself. Independence would provide the motivation. At some point Marcia would become totally responsible for this particular task, which mother could now safely delegate (S4).

Style 1–4 (the "one-four flop") and style 4–1 (the "four-one flop") are the most destructive patterns in business, families, interpersonal relationships, social systems, and therapy. In therapy, the 1–4 pattern exists when a client is in a highly structured setting (S1) and then released with little direction or support (S4). Psychiatric hospitalization followed by once a week outpatient therapy upon release is one example of this pattern. The 4–1 pattern, on the other hand, assumes that the client needs less direction than may actually be the case. When the client's problem remains unresolved or escalates, the therapist, recognizing the problem as one of direction, overreacts and rushes into an S1 stance. We often see this pattern around suicide issues in therapy, particularly with beginning therapists. An example of this is when a client has been expressing depression to an empathetic, understanding therapist for several weeks. When the client openly uses the word *suicide*, the therapist immediately suggests hospitalization. In both the "one-four flop" and the 'four-one flop" intermediate steps have been inappropriately omitted. Therapists who want to be more effective use treatment plans that gradually fill in the missing styles. Family aftercare programs in alcohol treatment are good examples of a gradual progression through the styles.

On occasion this disjunctive pattern can be used effectively. Some family therapists, for example, do little to support or direct a family while a diagnosis is being made and an intervention is being developed. The rationale in this pattern is based on the system therapist's appreciation for the strength of a family. The therapist's role is to discover which intervention will put the dysfunctional family on a helpful track. The intervention may be highly directive. To use such a 4–1 pattern requires great diagnostic and therapeutic skills and is frequently done in a setting in which teams of observers can assist the therapist in order to keep the therapist and the family on track.

The 3-1 or 1-3 disjunctive pattern can be characterized by, "When she was good, she was very, very good, but when she was bad, she was horrid." A 3-1 or 1-3 pattern suggests that the person is being very supportive sometimes and very directive at other times, without the combination that is a major element of style 2. This is the parent who barks an order at the child one minute (S1) and then says "I love you" the next (S3). What the child needs, and what is missing, is to be taught which behavior is unacceptable and which behavior is lovable (S2). By the same token, therapists who provide only support to the unable client are guilty of skipping a step in the therapy process. Good therapy, according to the ACT model, ensures an intermediate S2 approach. The therapist would help the client to learn the behavior necessary to complete the task.

"I taught you, now you're on your own." This is the statement that characterizes the 2-4 disjunctive pattern. This pattern is strong on selling or teaching but lacks the intermediate supportive S3 behavior that helps make a smooth transition from teaching to delegating. Intensive, instructional programs that incorporate little or no follow-up exemplify the 2-4 pattern. These settings increase the likelihood that some clients will not follow through. Some of the weight loss and intensive residential programs for changing life-style habits fall into this category. In some life-style programs, for example, clients check into the program for several intensive weeks of physical monitoring, exercise, education, and healthful eating (S2). These clients leave the program willing and now able to eat healthy foods and exercise properly. But willing and newly able clients need to be supported by S3 behavior. If the client returns home without support (S4), the transition for the new habits and learning is extremely rough. It is not unusual, therefore, for these clients to quickly resume their former habits. Some programs attempt to overcome this obstacle by having participants come in pairs so that they can provide the S3 support to one another for the transition to "back home" habits.

Less programmatic examples of a 2–4 process result from seminars and time-limited structured groups where significant amounts of both structure and support are provided, followed by termination. In designing such programs, the ACT model would recommend building in S3 behavior. For example, a six-week structured assertiveness group could allot time each session during which participants reported on their progress—on how the content of the group was applied in the past week. This would give the leader and the group members the opportunity to support and coach one another in the application and transfer of learning. The addition of S3 time (the sharing) may mean that the group has less S2 time to learn content. But ACT would suggest that this use of a transition style might ensure that the content learned is really used.

The 4–2 pattern can be characterized as delegate and remediate. Practitioners with a 4–2 pattern may need to monitor a tendency to set up therapeutic situations in such a way that the client flounders and fails—not from the client's insistence to go it alone but from the therapist's failure to support the client's development systematically with the appropriate S3 behavior.

While the ACT model prefers that therapy be a process of ordered progression through the appropriate quadrants for a given therapeutic task, there are times when the S4–S2 pattern can be used effectively with clients who overestimate their task-relevant ability. The client says, ''I can do it.'' The skeptical therapist says, ''Okay, give it a try. But we both agree that if there is a problem with this, you'll let me know so I can offer some suggestions to you.'' Premature attempts at independence are also familiar to parents. An S4–S2 parental stance may be effective in these situations as well. The overly ambitious child who wants to tackle a new activity without any instruction may be better off trying alone than having unwanted direction foisted upon him. If the child's ability is such that he succeeds, great! If this total delegation approach (S4) is unsuccessful, the S2 instruction is more likely to be received by a now willing learner.

This chapter began by discussing the structure of the TSI instrument and how you can use it in assessing your therapist style according to the ACT model. Style preference, style range, and style flexibility were defined, and we have discussed methods for scoring yourself in these three areas. Now that we have described the four preferred styles, as well as supporting styles, developing styles, adjacent styles, and disjunctive patterns, we are ready to discuss client readiness and its role in ACT.

5

※ ※ ※ ※ ※ ※ ※ ※ ※ ※ ※ ※ ※

Client Readiness:
The Key to Selecting
Therapeutic Style
and Form of Treatment

ACT is a developmental model in every sense of the word. Not only does the model tie the treatment plan to the client's developmental position, but it also views treatment as needing to be carried out in a stepwise, orderly, developmental fashion. Moreover, ACT sees the therapeutic process as being developmental—a process through which clients move toward higher levels of functioning. One of the key concepts of the ACT model is the concept of client readiness. Client readiness is an assessment about the client's developmental position regarding the therapeutic task in question.

There are three components to client readiness: competence, confidence, and motivation. This chapter examines each of these facets of developmental readiness in the context of basic developmental patterns evident in all humans. The problems that people bring to therapy can be conceptualized as setbacks or wrong turns along the path toward personal maturity. Personal maturity is defined as the appropriate level of readiness for that person to accomplish a particular set of life tasks. Therapy is an intervention designed to reorient the client on a productive developmental course.

88

Adaptive counseling and therapy gives the therapist a framework that aids in the diagnosis of the developmental difficulty, suggests the types of therapeutic interventions that will prove helpful for clients of various readiness levels, and suggests goals which, if accomplished, will become evidence of therapeutic progress. To explicate the concept of client task readiness, we need to describe the forces and directions involved in normal human development toward readiness.

Development: Making One's Way Through Life

One of the tasks of living is to make sense of the world we inhabit—the physical world around us, the social world constituted by our interactions with others, and the personal world each of us constructs within ourselves. The task of interpreting these worlds falls to our conscious minds. Consciousness employs idiosyncratic maps in order to understand experience. Korzybski (1950) pointed out that these maps of the world are not identical to the world itself but, rather, are only approximate representations of the worlds they seek to model. Individuals have differing models of the world, and it is these differences that are responsible for the tremendous variability in the ways humans choose to lead their lives. Differences in models may enrich our experience by offering us more choices, or they may impoverish our experience by limiting our ability to act effectively.

Bandler and Grinder (1975, p. 13) see an intimate connection between people's models of the world and the therapy process: "Our experience has been that, when people come to us in therapy, they typically come with pain, feeling themselves paralyzed, experiencing no choices or freedom of action in their lives. What we have found is not that the world is too limited or that there are no choices, but that these people block themselves from seeing those options and possibilities that are open to them since they are not available in their models of the world." The work of therapists might be defined as expanding their clients' models. Therapy highlights the parts of these models that enhance clients' experiences and the parts of these models that constrict and diminish them. Bandler and Grinder (1975,

p. 18) propose that all truly effective therapists share one trait: "They introduce changes in their clients' models which allow their clients more options in their behavior. What we see is that each of these wizards has a map or model for changing their clients' models of the world—i.e., a Meta-model which allows them to effectively expand and enrich their clients' models in some way that makes the clients' lives richer and more worth living."

Adaptive counseling and therapy holds that when a client's model becomes ineffective in some regard, the person operates at a low readiness level in that domain of action. To help the client develop, it is first necessary to establish the client's readiness for the therapeutic task at hand. Once this readiness level is assessed, ACT suggests a style of intervention (S1 through S4) that is theoretically optimal for inducing change and growth for that client. Adaptive counseling and therapy represents a type of metamodel whereby therapists can choose interventions to expand and enrich their clients' models.

What Is Readiness?

Chris Argyris (1957, 1962, 1964) contends that there are seven basic tasks people must accomplish in order to develop into mature adults. The following list summarizes these developmental challenges and characterizes the qualities that distinguish mature from immature functioning in any domain.

1. Change from a passive to a more active state.
2. Change from a state of dependency on others to relative independence.
3. Change from behaving in a few ways to acting in many ways.
4. Interests change from being erratic, shallow, and casual to mature, strong, and enduring.
5. Change from present-oriented time perspective to a perspective encompassing past, present, and future.
6. Change from solely subordinate relationships with others to relationships as equals or superiors.

7. Change from lack of a clear sense of self to a clearer sense of, and control of, self.

   To the extent that a person possesses those characteristics described as immature, that person might be considered unready in the domain and characteristics that are exhibited. If, in social situations, a person can behave in only one manner (Argyris's task 3)—that manner being very passive in nature (task 1) and rendering the person dependent on others (task 2)—the person would show low developmental readiness in the area of social skills. Argyris's developmental framework not only highlights the many ways in which one can show more ready versus less ready functioning, but it also immediately suggests alternative attitudes that could represent therapeutic goals: to develop a more active stance, to develop alternative behavior, to become more independent. Once again, we remind readers that the ACT model does not view readiness in a global sense. The person described here may well have a range of active behavior that allows him a great deal of independence at work or with his family. At work or at home, he may be at a more ready level of functioning.

   The seven developmental tasks are accomplished slowly, over a lifetime, and progress is often uneven and sometimes erratic. Readiness on a particular task at any age implies being somewhere within the normal range of accomplishments for people in that age group for activities relevant to that task. For example, the college freshman who describes adjustment problems related to leaving home for the first time is developmentally appropriate. The thirty-five-year-old bachelor who is anxious about moving out of his parents' home is developmentally inappropriate. Therapy would be indicated if a person's developmental readiness on a particular task dimension lagged far behind his or her peers.

   There are three impediments that might arrest one's progress toward desired goals. The three types of developmental difficulties are problems of competence, problems of confidence, and problems of motivation.

Problems of Competence

Problems of competence typically involve an inability to accomplish desired tasks or activities. When a client simply lacks the skills to accomplish a desired task, the difficulty is seen as one of competence. Considered developmentally, as children progress from less ready to more ready they are expected to master an enormous array of skills. If, for whatever reasons, a person fails to achieve the requisite skills that are necessary to enable him or her to accomplish a particular developmental task, the deficiency is viewed as a problem of competence.

The self-identified tasks of therapy and their concomitant competencies vary for different clients. John's grades, for example, do not reflect his aptitude. The counselor discovers he is so anxious about taking tests that he always scores below his ability. John lacks competence in test taking. Virginia is underachieving at college. However, her difficulties are related to the fact that her roommate keeps the stereo blasting and Virginia cannot concentrate on her studies. Virginia's lack of competence is related to asserting herself with her roommate or the residence hall advisers and learning about other options for studying such as the library. Pinpointing the competency problem has significant implications for treatment. Teaching John to use the library and exposing Virginia to relaxation training would not help either of them improve their grades.

Competency problems are broad. Even certain cognitive or conceptual deficiencies fall under the heading of competence problems. For example, neurolinguistic programming (Bandler and Grinder, 1975) and rational-emotive therapy (Ellis and Harper, 1961) teach clients cognitive skills to reframe or reconceptualize their backgrounds, experiences, and problems. Adaptive counseling and therapy views an enormous amount of the teaching that therapists undertake in therapy as efforts to aid clients in developing effective cognitive competencies.

Developing new cognitive competencies is often useful to aid clients in achieving a variety of developmental goals. A therapist may work to improve the way in which a client talks to herself about her ability to go places alone. The original task is to overcome her dependence on other people. Once mastering this therapeutic task, however, the client could well employ the skill to achieve goals in other developmental tasks. This ability to talk to oneself in a new way may have implications for becoming more active or developing better peer relationships. This generalization of skills is an example of the positive side effects of therapy that often go unnoticed and are almost impossible to capture in our research efforts to grasp the impact of psychotherapy.

Problems of Confidence

Often clients possess the requisite skills to achieve certain goals, but they find they are unable to bring themselves to do so. When clients are competent but unable to perform adequately, there are problems of confidence. Crises of confidence can be due to anxieties, insecurities, and general feelings of inadequacy. The picture is of a generally skilled person who is behaviorally paralyzed and incapable of using coping skills to achieve goals. Most of us have known people who were clearly able to make good decisions but whose lack of confidence in their ability to do so was paralyzing their decisiveness.

With problems of competence, the client does not have the skills to accomplish the target tasks. Confidence, on the other hand, refers to beliefs about the ability to perform tasks. Three distinct combinations of situations involving these two problems are noteworthy. First, there is the situation where the client is competent but lacks confidence. John, the anxious student, exemplifies this combination. He is a competent student, but he is so fearful he will not do well that his anxiety impedes his performance. In the second configuration, the client lacks necessary skills but feels confident that when those skills are learned implementation of them will be no problem. This client says, "I've never held a management position before, but I've always been able to work well with people so I'm sure I'll catch on." Competency, rather than confidence, is the issue. Finally, the client may not only lack the appropriate skills but may also believe that even if those skills were to be learned, he or she would not be capable of using them. "I've been offered the job of heading my department. I don't know anything about managing people and even if I did, I'm not sure I'd be very good at it anyway." This final case represents an instance where the client is both unconfident and incompetent. A somewhat different type of therapeutic approach is indicated for each of these three situations.

One might think of problems of confidence as representing situations where clients find themselves temporarily unable to bring about effective action in the service of their desired goals. Jerome Frank in *Persuasion and Healing* (1961) notes a similarity between therapy and religion in that both are capable of inspiring hope in the individual. This new hope provides the basis for a shift in belief that is the underpinning of therapeutic or religious change. Bandura's (1977) self-efficacy theory also speaks to the clients' confidence that they will be capable of achieving their desired therapeutic goals.

Problems of Motivation

Motivation problems are different from confidence problems because a client may be both competent and confident but may be *unwilling* to change. Clients may be unmotivated to change for a variety of reasons.

Clients are often unwilling to work toward their own therapeutic goals because of fear related to the process of change. While they may be experiencing psychological pain because of the difficulties that brought them to therapy, venturing into the unknown of a therapeutic solution is often frightening. Marriage therapists see couples every day who are miserable but who resist either behavior change or divorce. The nagging husband may know how to stop berating his wife for keeping a messy house and he may have the confidence that he could stop nagging if he so chose, but he is not willing to change his behavior. Perhaps he fears the house will get so messy that he will have to clean it himself. Perhaps he is angry with his wife about another issue and finds it less threatening to yell about the mess. Or perhaps he is unmotivated to stop nagging, because at least when they argue they are involved with one another. The wife, for her part, may know how to be a better housekeeper and may not lack confidence in this regard but for one reason or another is unwilling to be less messy. Perhaps she likes to use her time in some other way. Perhaps she too is angry at her husband about something else and punishes him by not cleaning house. Or perhaps she is afraid that if she tidies up the house, her husband will notice a more serious marital problem. At the least, both husband and wife are familiar with their present pattern of interaction and may be frightened about the potential outcome of a new, untested pattern. It is the fear of change that makes some people unwilling to change.

Other people are unmotivated to change because change is hard work. The anecdotal literature is replete with examples of clients who come to therapy with the misconception that the therapist can somehow work a magical cure which can remove their problem. When confronted with the reality that therapy is often an arduous, painful process, they sometimes realize that they are unwilling to assume the challenge of changing and thus must live with their problem. Clients can be motivated to seek therapy but still be unmotivated to change in therapy. This may be one of the reasons for many premature client-initiated terminations in therapy.

Secondary gain is also related to problems of motivation in therapy. While psychological difficulties can be painful, they can also produce a wide range of pleasant consequences. Disturbed people may be showered with nurturance, for example, and excused from responsibility. The changing of a psychologically maladaptive life-style has implications far beyond simply losing the psychological problem itself. As the implications of changing become progressively clear to the client, he or she may actually become less motivated to change.

A final general category of motivation problems stems from the fact that many clients are in therapy because their behavior is troubling to others, not necessarily to themselves. A broad array of disorders, from antisocial personality disorders to the acting out associated with adolescent adjustment difficulties, can bring clients to therapy because others are compromised by their behavior. Society finds their difficulty much more troubling than they do. In such instances, the client's lack of immediate motivation to change represents one of the first hurdles the therapist must overcome.

Therapists need to be cautious of clients' self-assessment of their developmental problem. For example, most children quickly learn that it is more socially acceptable to claim "I don't know how to tie my shoes" than to say "I don't feel like doing the work involved in tying my shoes." One is more likely to obtain help by claiming incompetence than by expressing a lack of motivation. Therefore some people have also learned to ask for professional help by expressing problems of motivation as problems of competence. Therapists must be able to tease out the differences between real competence problems and motivation problems masquerading as competence difficulties.

Levels of Analysis

Having considered the question of client readiness, we turn now to the treatment options available to the therapist. When considering treatment options, the ACT model can be expanded to include two levels of analysis. The first level, microanalysis, involves the specific treatment techniques and styles employed by the therapist. Thus far we have been talking only about this level of analysis. But adaptive counseling and therapy can also be used at a level of macroanalysis in which the form or setting of treatment is decided. The prescribed form of treatment is based on the client's general level of functioning and the treatment goals. Figure 5 illustrates four forms of intervention in terms of the ACT model. At the level of macroanalysis for treatment planning, the following distinctions about forms of treatment can be made.

F1: Institutional. The most structured setting for treatment is *institutional*. Persons whose overall level of functioning is such that they are not currently capable of independent functioning need the structure and direction of an institutional setting that provides continuous monitoring and direction. The need for that

Figure 5. Macrolevel of Analysis: Four Forms of Treatment.

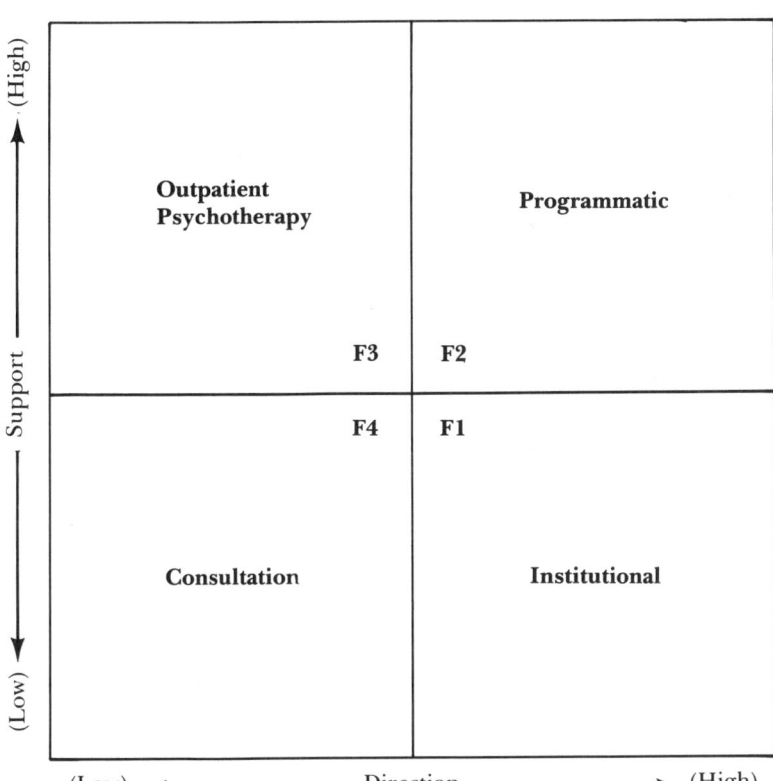

level of structure and support may be quite temporary, as in the case of various acute disturbances, or very long term, as for the profoundly mentally retarded who may never function outside an institutional environment. Hospitals are the primary institutional treatment setting for mental health problems.

F2: Programmatic. The *programmatic* form of treatment involves much more intensive structuring of time and activities than is possible on a once-a-week outpatient basis, but it involves persons who are able to function more independently than those for whom an institutional setting is indicated. Programs such as day or evening nonhospital care structure and direct much of a person's activity while providing moderate to high amounts of support. Other examples of programmatic forms of treatment might include daily involvement in a stress management program with programmed activities in relaxation, nutrition, exercise, and biofeedback or regular participation in Alcoholics Anonymous. There has been a phenomenal growth in self-help programs in the last twenty years. The best of these programs provide both structure and support to their members.

F3: Outpatient Psychotherapy. The *outpatient* form of treatment is the form of all the treatments at the level of microanalysis. Outpatient psychotherapy falls in the F3 quadrant because the form of therapy is basically one of high support and low to moderate direction. In order to benefit from a weekly outpatient visit, clients must have their lives in some semblance of order at least with respect to basic survival needs and physiological safety. All styles of outpatient treatment require that the client play a major role in implementing the therapist's directives.

F4: Consultation. The fourth form of treatment, *consultation*, is appropriate for persons who have the capacity, motivation, and support to carry out decisions made as part of a brief consultative relationship. Many of us use office calls to a physician's office in this way. After we present our symptoms, the physician diagnoses the problem and prescribes some treatment regimen that we are willing and able to carry out.

Use of Treatment Forms in
Progressive and Regressive Cycles

Within a developmental framework, there is an assumption that growth is in an upward direction. Backsliding, then, is also a developmental problem. Consider the client who has made good progress in adjusting to divorce. She has been less depressed, more socially active, and more self-confident than several months earlier. But then, gradually, she begins to show minor depressive symptoms, stops attending church, and expresses increased self-doubt in the therapy sessions. In such cases the course of treatment recommended by ACT is somewhat different from the suggested therapeutic approach for someone who has never before attained that level of readiness.

One of the therapist's assessment tasks is to distinguish between two kinds of developmental cycles. These cycles can be either progressive or regressive. In a progressive cycle, the client advances toward higher levels of readiness. In a regressive cycle, the client once functioned at a more ready level but has since slipped to a lower readiness level. The treatment procedures for two frequent problems illustrate progress through the various forms of treatment. The first, treatment for chemical dependency, illustrates the use of various treatment forms in a progressive cycle. The second, treatment for obesity, exemplifies the use of treatment forms in a regressive cycle.

Chemical Dependency Treatment Sequence. Because of the denial frequently involved in chemical dependency and the problems attendant to physical addictions, treatment programs usually begin with an inpatient hospital stay, often lasting twenty-eight days (F1). This period may include detoxification, confronting the client's denial of the problem, education, group treatment, and Alcoholics Anonymous meetings. The environmental controls of a hospital setting, which limit access to alcohol, are necessary because the person has been unable and unwilling to control his or her drinking. Many such programs are now involving the client's support system (spouse, family, friends, employer) as part of this stage of the treatment process.

After the client completes the inpatient part of the program, he or she moves into the aftercare elements of a programmatic format (F2). In aftercare, clients have more responsibility for their own behavior and there are fewer controls over access to alcohol. However, the programmatic involvement is significant, intensive, and supportive. It usually includes frequent Alcoholics Anonymous meetings, group therapy, and individual, marital, or family counseling. The duration of aftercare programs may vary. Some are structured to have a specific conclusion while others are more open-ended. As the client moves to the successful completion of the programmatic form of treatment, the frequency, duration, and intensity of the programmatic contacts may be reduced (F3). The client is now able to determine, for example, when an AA meeting is needed and to initiate marital counseling if new problems arise or old problems resurface. Finally, the client may develop sufficient direction and support internally and environmentally so that no organized treatment is now necessary (F4).

This treatment for chemical dependency is a good example of the importance of moving through the sequencing of treatment one step at a time. Early in the progressive cycle, each treatment step pulls back just a little on direction and moves up just a little on support. Such sequencing is the process of moving from S1 or F1 to S2 or F2. In later phases of treatment in the progressive cycle, each treatment step continues to pull back on direction and now also pulls back on support. Eventually, the hope is that the client will be self-supporting and self-directing. Figure 6 illustrates this sequence.

We believe that alcohol treatment plans that do not involve some aspects of all four quadrants will be less successful than those that do. Outpatient insight-oriented treatment, without the addition of more structured forms of treatment, may have insufficient structure and directiveness to confront the alcoholic and begin remediation of the drinking problem. Similarly, hospital time to dry out without subsequent programmatic support and structure may lead to the revolving-door pattern that typifies the one-four flop—high structure immediately followed by no structure or support.

While one of the authors was an intern at a VA hospital, he witnessed and participated in the one-four flop pattern repeatedly. Many of the patients were institutionalized in the sense that they accepted having most of life's day-to-day decisions made for them. He paraphrased the hospital's stance in this manner:

> The patients don't need to decide when to get up—
> we tell them. They don't need to decide what to
> eat nor do they work to prepare it—they just go
> to the dining hall at noon for lunch. Frequently the
> patient's goal seems to be to remain hospitalized

Figure 6. Sequencing of Treatment One Step at a Time.

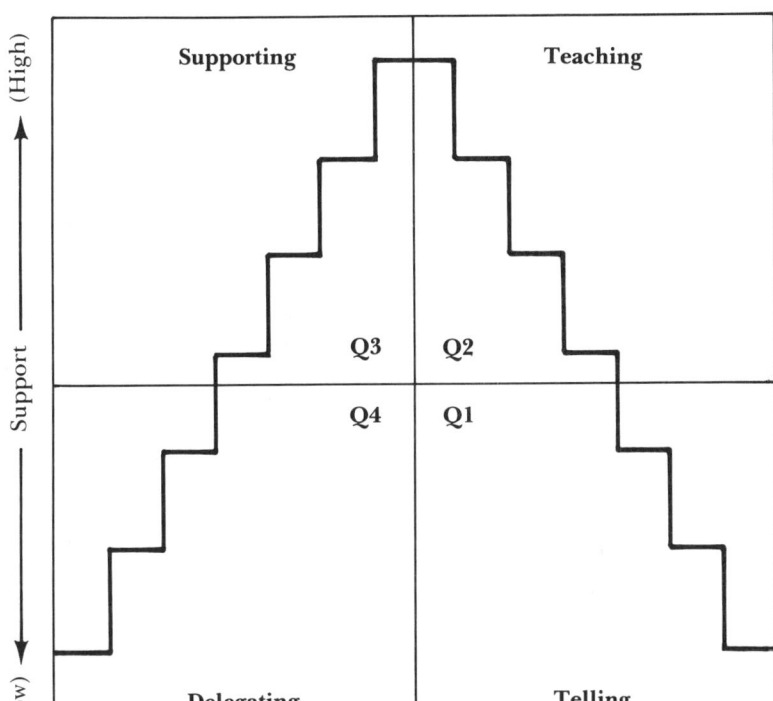

rather than go home. We work at individual and
group therapy, chemotherapy, OT, RT, IT, and
any other T anyone can think of to patch up their
damaged psyches. When no longer actively psychotic, clients are sent home with no real transi-
tional treatment. Frequently, within a relatively
short period of time, the revolving door reveals the
same patients, "crazy as a bed bug," and the process starts anew.

Weight Control Treatment Sequence. A second problem that
illustrates the various forms and sequence of treatments is weight
control. Many of us control our weights by using only the

consultation quadrant (F4). We consult the scale, say, *"oops!"* and then skip dessert or run a few extra miles. In this manner we maintain our weight within the range we find acceptable. If consultation with our scale, mirror, or apparel is not sufficient to maintain our weight at an acceptable level, we may go on a diet. This pattern represents the implementation of self-directed structure. We may also enlist the support of the immediate environment by announcing our intentions, seeking advice, and having a friend hurry us past the ice cream shop (F3). The involvement with higher levels of support and a little more direction carries people to programs such as Nutrisystems which provide both high structure and high support (F2). These programs not only tell clients what to eat but even provide them with the food. If people cannot control their eating on an outpatient programmatic basis, they may enroll in an institutional program (F1). These institutional settings range from plush "fat farms" to stark hospital settings. Within the institution, the degree of directiveness and control is great and predominantly external. At the extreme of this continuum are procedures that involve stapling the stomach or removing intestine so that it becomes physically difficult or even impossible to eat too much. Control is totally in the hands of the therapeutic change agent in F1 programs.

Weight control has been a regressive problem for many in that the individual is successful for a while but tends to regress over time and in the absence of treatment. When treating someone who is regressing, the same one-step-at-a-time approach used in cycles is appropriate. In regressive cycles, however, the best approach is to get just behind the person who is falling backward in order to nudge them forward and back on course. The person who had been going regularly to Weight Watchers but is no longer attending may begin to gain a few pounds without the reinforcement of the group. To stop this regressive cycle she may need only to return to the Weight Watchers group a time or two (an illustration of getting just behind where the regressing client is and nudging forward). She would not need to enter a hospital program immediately (an illustration of getting many steps behind the regressing client) nor should she insist on doing it all herself (an illustration of moving ahead of the regression).

In the treatment of a weight problem, part of the assessment might involve asking questions like these: What forms of treatment have been tried before, and how successful have they been? How much structure and support were used in past treatments? How capable and willing is the client to control his or her food intake? What form of treatment is most likely to produce positive results while maintaining a maximum of internal structure and support? The answers to such queries will determine the most appropriate style of treatment.

This chapter has been concerned with the client's readiness and how it can best be determined. Apart from discovering the client's readiness related to the therapeutic task at hand, the therapist also needs to assess whether the client's movement is in a progressive or a regressive cycle. In the last part of this chapter, we have tried to expand the reader's view of the implications of ACT theory. By applying the ACT model, therapists and counselors can not only determine the best style for optimum treatment but also the best form of treatment as well. In so doing, it becomes apparent that the context in which therapeutic intervention is nested often represents a significant part of the total treatment package. Before moving on to further assessment issues, we present some clinical applications of ACT in Chapter Six.

6

🀫 🀫 🀫 🀫 🀫 🀫 🀫 🀫 🀫 🀫 🀫 🀫 🀫

Choosing Therapeutic
Style and Treatment
in Actual Practice:
Case Studies

Only the rarest clients present us with a simple problem. The various people who require our help generally are dealing with a range of problems that fall at many points along a continuum of complexity. One of the values of the ACT model is its ability to help therapists develop a treatment plan for the range of clients with whom they must work. To apply the ACT model in treatment planning requires that the therapist, often in tandem with the client, break down even the most complex situation into separate therapeutic tasks. The client's readiness for each of the tasks is then assessed. Using this procedure, it is possible to develop a treatment plan for all kinds of clients with all kinds of problems. In this chapter we will look at two different cases to illustrate the role that ACT can play in applied psychotherapy. Together these cases represent the range of situations in which most therapists might find themselves. The first case discusses treatment in short-term psychotherapy; the second describes a long-term, complex, and very intense therapy situation.

Before turning to the case discussion, we must remind you that ACT is an adjunctive model for therapy. It does not provide a conceptual base for understanding human behavior.

Instead it allows therapists to use their own conceptual framework for understanding the client's behavior while providing an augmenting dimension that helps in the selection of the best method for enhancing the client's potential for change. In our case discussions, we try to demonstrate just how a therapist's own conceptual orientation and the ACT model can fit together.

Karen: A Matter of Confidence

Karen came into therapy a year after she had graduated from college. She was obviously quite bright and capable but very quiet, very shy, and generally unsure of herself. She was employed as a social worker and despised her job, feeling unchallenged in a job that was filled with petty bureaucratic tasks. Karen focused a lot on her self-perception of social ineptitude. She believed that she lacked the forcefulness to make things happen—both in her own life and in the lives of people who meandered through the agency where she worked. She described herself as depressed and without purpose or direction. When her therapist asked, "If I had a magic wand, what would you want to have happen if I waved it over you?," Karen replied, "I'd turn into an outgoing life-of-the-party who was totally self-assured. I would know exactly what I wanted to be doing with my life."

In terms of Karen's interpersonal behavior, the therapist chose to relabel Karen's problem as one of "not appreciating herself" rather than accepting Karen's need to change into a different kind of person. In this way, the problem became a confidence problem. Since Karen accepted the therapist's reframing of the problem, there was no question of willingness. Obviously competence was not a problem. Karen already had the ability to be the way she was.

With the problem so restated, the therapist saw the task as one of needing to teach Karen to value herself and providing Karen with a general perspective about people in order to help her see how her social behavior fit into the broader picture. This "teaching" is an S2 therapist style. The following excerpt from one therapy session shows how the therapist handled the issue of Karen's confidence related to social behavior:

Karen:	I'm furious with myself. I went to this party last weekend and I just stood around like a—a dead fish. I just couldn't think of anything to say.
Therapist:	Tell me a little more about the way things went. It sounds like you were sitting alone . . . frozen. [*Information gathering*]
Karen:	Uh, well, not exactly. I mean I was either part of a group that was talking or sitting with just one or two other people.
Therapist:	So nobody seemed to be avoiding you? [*Information gathering*]
Karen:	Oh, no! It's just that I do most of the listening and the other people talk. I feel so inadequate. I, um, I just can't seem to think of anything really witty or interesting to say.
Therapist:	So. You're a good listener? [*Reframing the problem*]
Karen:	I guess. People tell me that sometimes.
Therapist:	Thank goodness there are some good listeners in the world. Can you imagine how awful it would be if everyone just wanted to talk and nobody wanted to listen? [*Teaching a new perspective (support)*]
Karen:	But I'm so quiet.
Therapist:	I've noticed that. But I would call you "laid back." It's refreshing to be with someone who doesn't chatter around. Your style is, um, kind of relaxing rather than making a person jumpy. [*Teaching a new perspective (support)*]
Karen:	Well, you're just trying to make me feel better. I doubt that others would say that.

Therapist:	I haven't heard you say you have no friends. [*Information checking*]
Karen:	That's true. I have a lot of friends. But they all seem to find it easy to carry on a conversation.
Therapist:	So most of your friends talk a lot and seek you out because you're such a good listener? [*Reframing*]
Karen:	Maybe.
Therapist:	Karen, I want you to remember this the next time you are with your friends. I think they need you precisely because you are the way you are. Can you keep that in mind? [*Assigning (direction)*]
Karen:	I'll try, but . . .
Therapist:	I need to interrupt you. I'm asking you to do something for me and for yourself. The next time you go to a party I'd like you to remember that your quietness is important. Okay? [*Assigning (direction)*]
Karen:	Okay.

Throughout the therapy process there was strong support for Karen to remain as she was. The client needed the therapist's appreciation in order to begin to value herself. The therapeutic task was defined as needing to teach Karen new ways to view herself and her situation. The therapist believed that once Karen learned to appreciate herself, she would be able to apply her new-found confidence in social situations. (You can see how the therapist's theoretical notions about change affected the therapeutic goal.) At times, Karen's unwillingness required that the therapist provide strong direction in order to help Karen try things that would boost her confidence. The choice of an S2 therapist stance ensured that support would be an ongoing part of the therapeutic process no matter how much or how little direction Karen needed at particular times.

Apart from the therapy goal related to Karen's feelings about herself in social situations, there was also a career issue for this client. The therapist assessed Karen as willing, able, and reasonably confident to consider a career change. An S3 career exploration process that occasionally involved some S2 teaching about career possibilities and requirements for various careers was incorporated in the therapy.

Karen was in therapy a little less than a year. By the time of termination, she had decided to return to college and take some science courses in order to apply to medical school— something she had always wanted to do but had been afraid to try. Her academic history, the therapist's assessment, and past test scores all suggested that Karen was a viable candidate for acceptance to a medical school. And, in fact, Karen did eventually complete her medical education. At last account, she had just finished the second year of a psychiatric residency at a prestigious training facility. Her confidence was excellent. She now could appreciate herself as a person both in terms of personal qualities and in terms of a belief in her own abilities. Karen was finding significant satisfaction in the intellectual stimulation of psychiatry and in its clinical application. She laughed when she told the therapist, "Well, I'm still finding places where listening is a valued commodity."

Since Karen's abilities were manifold, her therapist decided not to work on ability issues. But assessing Karen's problem as one of confidence, as one of needing to learn to appreciate herself, does not mean that there is only one appropriate treatment plan. Not all therapists who would diagnose Karen's problem as a lack of self-esteem would necessarily conceptualize the problem in the same way as this therapist did. Different therapists have differing perspectives about the etiology of human behavior. For example, a clinician who believed that Karen's lack of confidence was the result of internalized self-defeating childhood messages might decide that spending time with Karen discussing her childhood would have treatment value for defusing these inappropriate messages. There are, then, readiness questions related to the therapeutic task of discussing Karen's childhood. Would Karen be willing to spend therapy in this manner, or is she expecting something different? How good is her recall? How confident is Karen that she can help the therapist retrace her past? The way in which the therapist sets about the task of gathering childhood information will be determined by the answers to these questions. Methods of treatment might include anything from a detailed questionnaire (highly directive, little support) to conversations (varying direction and support) to the client maintaining a journal of thoughts about her childhood (no direction, no support). We think you can see that if Karen was low in willingness, ability, and confidence to review her childhood, asking her to keep a journal would have little likelihood of success. If, on the other hand, she was ready, willing, and able to discuss her childhood, the detailed questionnaire would not be appropriate.

Clearly, Karen's problem might have been conceptualized differently by a third therapist. Had the focus been on Karen's ability to be a more gregarious person, an area in which Karen was lacking, the treatment plan would have revolved around skill building. If the therapist decides to approach the issue of self-esteem by helping the client develop new skills, these questions must be answered: How motivated is the client for change in these areas? What is her current skill level? What is her confidence level? Even assuming the therapist decides that social skills or assertiveness training is the treatment of choice, there are still a number of style options in the presentation of the training. Whether the therapist assigns or asks the client to assign herself an assertiveness task, for example, will be the result of an ACT assessment—the answer to questions related to motivation, ability, and confidence.

Whatever one's theoretical orientation, assessing the client on willingness, ability, and confidence vis-à-vis the specific therapeutic task will help move treatment from a conceptual set of ideas (she needs to improve her self-esteem) to a systematic plan for change (what treatment plan will help her to improve her self-esteem?). We know that this brief review of Karen's case does not do justice to the intricacy of a therapy process. For illustration, we have focused on the two most significant elements of her treatment. Many more strands were woven into the fabric of the case, however—Karen's relationship with her alcoholic father, questions she had pertaining to a live-in boyfriend, her feminist feelings, and her relationship to her women friends. But we chose Karen's case because it easily demonstrates the reduction of the treatment process into separate tasks and goals. Karen did not have a significant pathological component to her problem. She was diagnosed as having an adjustment reaction with depressed affect. The treatment plan was relatively uncomplicated and the outcome was excellent from both Karen's and the therapist's perspective.

But not every case is so easy to assess and treat as Karen's case. And not every case has so successful an outcome. Many of us also see clients for whom treatment is significantly more complex—whose level of disturbance requires a great range in style and different forms of therapy based on the macroanalysis of the client's problems. ACT can be especially helpful in such treatment planning because it provides a structure within which important clinical decisions can be made.

Debra: The Woman Who Had No Childhood

Debra represents the other end of the treatment continuum—a long-term psychotherapy client with very severe problems. Debra required the full range of therapist styles and the full range of treatment forms. In Debra's case, outpatient psychotherapy in and of itself would not have been sufficient.

An understanding of Debra's background is necessary in order to discern the value of treatment styles and treatment forms in the management of her case. The therapist, Carol, recognized immediately that therapy with Debra would be both long term and taxing. In fact, one of the early treatment decisions Carol faced was the question of whether or not to accept a case of this magnitude. In the poignant first meeting, Debra was obviously a client who resonated with depression and despair. Carol was greeted by a thirty-three-year-old, significantly overweight woman, who dragged into the office and sank heavily into the chair. Her words were carefully chosen; her voice quiet; the pace slow. Debra was direct, concise, and obviously bright, but her gloom was oppressive. She said she was seeking counseling because of depression, feelings of emptiness, and poor interpersonal relationships.

Early in therapy, Carol asked Debra what she thought about the possibility of abuse in her childhood. Debra claimed almost no memory of her childhood prior to her eleventh birthday. Nevertheless, she added, down deep she believed she had been abused. Too many things in her life that seemed inexplicable would make perfect sense if, in fact, there had been childhood incest. She had been reading a lot about incest and abuse and definitely wanted to explore the possibility, although she admitted to anxiety about the process. Debra appeared to be highly motivated to pursue this avenue of therapy. (During therapy, Debra uncovered memories of a childhood filled with physical, sexual, and psychological abuse.)

Debra's history included two prior therapeutic experiences, both of which were most unsatisfactory. Her first "therapy" involved a sexual relationship with her therapist, a man old enough to be her father. This relationship unfortunately mirrored her sexual betrayal by her father—an authority figure who should have been, but was not, trustworthy. The therapy and the relationship ended when the therapist moved to another community.

Debra terminated her second therapy experience because she questioned the therapist's competence. The therapist, a middle-aged female, responded to Debra's raising of questions about the possibility of childhood incest by insisting that Debra's thoughts were either the result of an active imagination or some type of paranoia. Just as the first therapy experience mirrored the sexual betrayal by her father, so Debra's second therapy experience seemed to reenact the negation of trust that occurred in the original mother-daughter relationship. Neither Debra's mother nor her female therapist was able to protect her appropriately.

Carol's initial clinical hypothesis, one that tested out over time, included a diagnosis of borderline personality disorder. Carol had seen a number of similar clients over the years. The incest hypothesis was rooted in Carol's recognition of a clinical profile that was all too familiar. One component of this profile is a lack of childhood memory. In addition to amnesia about her childhood, Debra exhibited several other characteristics common to a history of sexual abuse. For one thing, she, like similar clients, described herself as exhibiting "crazy" behavior. One example of her "crazy" behavior was excessive rumination about vaginal and rectal disorders while repeatedly refusing medical attention. Therapy, for women like Debra, generally enables them to recognize that these symptoms are not randomly crazy but rather are rooted in a long-forgotten real-life antecedent—a memory so unpleasant that it has been repressed and forgotten. Although Debra was willing to participate in the task of exploring the roots of her fear of doctors, she was not at all willing, in the early phases of treatment, to participate in any behavior change as far as medical treatment was concerned.

Another characteristic Debra shared with other abused borderline women was self-abuse. She repeatedly cut herself in the genital area and occasionally on the bottoms of her feet. Debra's obesity matched another part of the profile of abuse. Eating disorders are prevalent in incest victims. Debra described a hope that being fat would protect her from sexual advances as well as help her fight off unwanted attacks, a not unusual belief among sexual assault victims. She began gaining weight at age five, an age that later turned out to be the age at which the sexual abuse began. Debra's obesity also seemed to be a metaphorical statement about lack of control. Children who are trapped in desperate situations learn early how little control they have over their own destinies and carry these control issues into later life.

Like many other severely abused borderline women, Debra was an unusually bright and successful professional. Intelligence may well be the factor that makes these women borderline cases rather than hopelessly psychotic. In her professional life, Debra needed little guidance. Her readiness related to career issues was excellent. She was a willing, able, and confident professional.

In other areas of her life, however, her readiness level was low. Aside from her professional identity, Debra had little sense of herself. She would often say, "I don't have any idea who Debra is. I feel like a nothing . . . like a no one." Her theme was one of feeling empty without an internal core that she could identify as self. Debra suffered from a profound identity disturbance.

Debra's complete history took several years to reconstruct due to the childhood amnesia with which she began therapy. She was the youngest of three children and the only daughter born to stern, working-class, German-Catholic parents. Both parents were from large, disturbed families where a history of abuse and incest connected the generations, although it was veiled under staunch religiosity. Debra's childhood was characterized by a total lack of emotional and physical protection. Verbal, sexual, and physical abuse from both parents began early and continued in one form or another until she left home. Sexual abuse by her father included oral, anal, and vaginal intercourse that was often coupled with sadistic physical abuse. Her mother actively participated in the physical, verbal, and sexual abuse. During some of the early childhood years, her mother also solicited other adult male partners for Debra. Much of the solicited sexual activity was of a sadistic nature. Debra was further isolated because her siblings totally rejected her, a not unusual response directed toward scapegoated incest victims according to Mandelbaum (1977).

Debra attended Catholic schools all her life, where she was an excellent student. School was her sanctuary, although she eventually expressed great anger at the school for ignoring the evidence of her abuse and not protecting her. The same anger was later directed at neighbors and extended family. No one protected her; no one in the family, no one at school, no one in the neigborhood. Survival in this environment was not easy. Debra accomplished it by blocking both the pain and the reality of what was happening. It is here that her intelligence helped her—her mind was her refuge.

The sexual abuse in all forms stopped at age eleven, perhaps because of the threat of her burgeoning womanhood. Her large and growing body size made her a less physically helpless victim. It may also be that the older she grew, the more her parents feared that she would be capable of telling or protesting. The next few years she was outwardly functional but inwardly numbed, scarred, and damaged. During her first year of college she began to lose control of her feelings. In fear, she first sought therapy. Her early therapy experiences left a lot to be desired, but they apparently patched her sufficiently to reactivate the blocking and numbing survival mechanisms. In this way, she was able to limp along for the next ten years. When she contacted Carol for therapy, it was not because she was out of control but because she wanted to "stop just existing and find a life worth living." Debra entered therapy extremely willing to participate in the therapeutic process. She was seeking therapy very much on her own initiative.

The treatment plan was structural rather than adaptational (Gordon and Beresin, 1983). Carol's plan was not merely to help Debra adjust to her situation, but rather to work on rebuilding Debra's personality structure. In general, therapy involved an intensive reparenting process (Cohen, 1984; Minuchin, 1974). The major tasks of therapy included building trust in the therapeutic relationship as a foundation of the developmental process, retrieval of childhood memory, expression of affect (particularly anger and grief), integration of the splitting process (Mahler, 1971; Fairbairn, 1952), and helping the client develop a differentiated identity. Each major task was composed of many smaller subtasks—for example, recollecting the various pieces of her puzzled past became a series of tasks. The course of treatment was much like a rich tapestry of interwoven threads. It was not as if each task was an isolated segment of a process.

Such a treatment plan required tremendous therapeutic resources. There were several years of intense outpatient therapy that required significant range and flexibility on the part of the therapist. In addition to the outpatient psychotherapy, treatment involved regular use of partial hospitalization and inpatient treatment in a unit that provided intense programmatic therapy. Integrating outpatient therapy, hospitalization, and partial hospitalization required a macrolevel of analysis—one that looked at desired forms of treatment. Debra's treatment plan, in order to be successful, involved a commitment of time and energy and a team united in the treatment process.

A detailed description of the course of treatment illustrates both the use of the macrolevel of analysis and decisions related to therapist style in complex cases. The first phase of treatment was once-a-week outpatient therapy. At the macrolevel of analysis, treatment was of the F3 form. During this period, memory barriers were slowly breaking down, Debra's history was emerging, and the therapeutic relationship was developing. The therapist's style in the early phase was a combination of S2 and S3. Debra's willingness to cooperate in her therapy allowed the therapist to be very supportive. This supportive stance also permitted the therapeutic relationship to develop. The therapist needed to be more directive, mostly in those areas where Debra's competence and confidence were lacking. For example, it was almost impossible at first for Debra to remember any part of her early childhood. She did not have the faintest idea how to remember, and she was petrified about what the memories might be and how she would react to them. Carol, therefore, added a significant direction component while continuing to be supportive. Relaxation, hypnosis, and specific verbal questions and prods all helped to direct the memory retrieval process. In session, with direction from Carol, Debra easily fell into a trancelike child state and it was in this state that memory retrieval and affective behavior occurred. The splitting common to borderline clients (Kernberg, 1975; Mahler, 1971) became obvious. The childlike Debra cried and had feelings. Sometimes she would say to Carol, "I wish you were my mommy." The adult Debra operated mostly at a cognitive level. Only late in treatment, as the previously split child and adult began to integrate, could Debra permit herself to confess to Carol, "I wish my mother had been more like you."

With clients such as Debra, support from the therapist involves total trustworthiness. Debra had never known the meaning of trust. If her development was to continue, this missing link had to be supplied. Because trust is so crucial, the therapist must not make promises that cannot be fulfilled and likewise must behave consistently with what is promised. When Carol would leave town, for example, Debra would plead, "Promise me you'll come back." Carol was always careful to respond, "As long as I have something to say about things, you can be sure I'll be back. If I don't get back, we'll both have something to be upset about because it will mean the plane crashed or something." Carol did not want to make promises related to acts of God that she might not be able to keep. The cost of such a total promise could prove to be too much for Debra. Carol was careful to remind Debra that there would be times when she might inadvertently hurt Debra. "That's bound to happen in any relationship. But you can be sure it would never be my intention to hurt or harm you in any way." Such a case requires extensive therapist care and commitment.

The pain triggered by Debra's retrieval of some of her childhood memories created a strong suicidal depression and an inability to function that set the stage for the second phase of treatment, a two-week intensive hospitalization. The primary therapeutic task during this period of treatment was one of assisting Debra in the expression of grief and anger. The intensity of this task, as well as Debra's lack of experience in expressing her feelings, required the structure and direction available with hospitalization, an F1 form of treatment. In one sense, Debra's functioning was regressing as a result of a treatment that created the return of repressed memories. As functioning regressed, it was necessary to adjust the form of treatment so that the direction which Debra was no longer able to provide herself was provided by the treatment setting. Within an F1 form, however, there can be a wide range and much diversity in therapeutic style.

Treatment during this phase was enhanced by an inpatient therapy team that had a great deal of experience with patients like Debra. Inpatient treatment included sessions with the psychiatrist and various staff in individual and group settings. Individual sessions used therapy from all four styles depending on the specific therapeutic task and Debra's readiness level. Twice a day, for example, a brief S2 treatment was employed to desensitize Debra to certain "trigger" words. In such desensitization therapy, a structure is provided but the client has some responsibility for how the structure is used. Debra developed a list of words that had been very upsetting in the past—words that triggered an emotional response which often led to inappropriate behavior. Obviously the choice of the words was left to Debra, who provided the direction for what transpired during desensitization. Support was provided by the staff member who provided the therapy. During the desensitization process, the staff member continued to bombard Debra with the trigger word while encouraging her to express the feelings elicited by that word.

Similarly, psychodrama is an S2 therapy. There is a structure to psychodrama, but what can take place within that structure is variable. Staff provide support and direction when necessary. Debra attended psychodrama twice a week while hospitalized. During this time, she used psychodrama mostly as an observer. While attendance was mandatory (very directive), Debra was not required to be the protagonist. Staff assessed that she was not yet ready for that role. The ACT model would support postponing an aspect of treatment for which a client is currently unready but is likely to be receptive to at a later date. Sequencing of therapeutic tasks is critical. More will be said about this in the following chapter.

Inpatient treatment also included regular group therapy, guided imagery sessions, assertiveness training, and various recreational therapies. Most of these treatments fall primarily into an S2 category within an F1 setting. The group therapy, which varied from S1 to S4 in style, was very important in providing an environment where Debra could begin to transfer the trust and intimacy she was developing in individual therapy to selected others.

After the hospital stay, outpatient therapy was increased to twice a week—again an F3 form by macroanalysis. The goal was to maintain the momentum by maximizing therapeutic contact. A second two-week hospitalization took place six months later, followed again by outpatient treatment. Throughout the time following the first hospitalization, Debra's therapy was augmented with four hours a week in partial hospitalization in an evening hospital setting. Participation in evening hospital is a programmatic form of treatment (F2). This combination of F2 and F3 treatment was necessary for Debra at that time since she was functioning well enough not to require full hospitalization but not well enough to participate only in outpatient psychotherapy. Partial hospitalization included psychodrama and group therapy with some of the staff and patients Debra had been involved with as an inpatient.

During the last year and a half of treatment, a slow process of therapeutic disengagement was formulated. Partial hospitalization was reduced to one night a week for several months and then phased out completely. Outpatient psychotherapy returned to a weekly basis. Gradually, Carol began discussing termination with Debra and together they planned for new support systems once therapy was over. Debra joined a community support group for incest victims and asked to be assigned a lay counselor through her church. Church involvement increased for Debra during this period—not only because she needed more outside support but also because she found herself with more and more time as the therapy process was winding down. When Debra forgot to keep two consecutive appointments, Carol read Debra's forgetfulness as an expression of her lessening dependency on therapy despite the ambivalence about separation from Carol. Debra's growing sense of herself was a harbinger of a growing identity and autonomy.

Several months before the conclusion of the treatment process, Debra spent several hours with a counselor who specialized in career planning. Debra felt she had some professional decisions to make. At the macrolevel of analysis, Debra was using the F4 consultative form of treatment. As a result of the career planning, Debra decided to take additional professional training. This training was intellectually stimulating for Debra but, in addition, her new skills gave her the opportunity to expand her professional role. This path eventually led Debra to a new job requiring a greater involvement with people. The new job appeared to be a signal that significant change had occurred. At one time Debra found isolation reinforcing. Now she wanted greater social involvement.

Debra's involvement in outpatient psychotherapy, partial hospitalization, full hospitalization, and career planning was directly related to her readiness level or functioning ability. The form of treatment varied systematically to match the client's need. When debilitating depression made Debra unwilling, unable, and unconfident, an F1 form of treatment was used. When Debra willingly approached career issues, an area of strength, an F4 treatment was the form of choice.

In retrospect, the goals of treatment were mostly achieved. Debra now knows her history. She has wept over it and been enraged about it. The child and the adult have been integrated, as has most of the splitting of the bad and the good introjections and projections. Debra recognizes that she can no longer categorize herself or others as all good or all bad. She is continuing to discover who she is and how she became who she is. She is more comfortable with herself and with other people. She acknowledges and copes with her inner conflicts rather than repressing them. Debra has developed several female friends. However, she still needs continual reassurance that she can trust people. There has been little progress in her relationships with men. When possible, she avoids them and what contact she does have is mostly unsuccessful. Issues of trust, sexuality, and social comfort are clearly unresolved where men are concerned. She showed little interest in working on these issues at the time of termination. In this area she lacked motivation, ability, and confidence.

Debra's personal therapeutic goal was to ''stop just existing and find a life worth living.'' Blocher (1966) believes that a counselor's central professional role involves the facilitation of human development. Perhaps, at some later stage, when Debra can risk again, she will choose to work in therapy on further developmental steps. In particular, Debra might benefit from an exploration of her contemporary relationship with her parents and siblings and an acceptance of her family of origin. Debra is angry at her family and chooses to avoid all contact with them. For now, Debra's anger is important. It was earned in one of the most painful ways imaginable and it was repressed too long. And Debra is tired. She wants a rest from therapy.

The ACT model has a broad range of clinical applicability. By pinpointing therapeutic tasks and assessing the client's readiness related to each of the tasks, a treatment plan can be formulated. As a therapy situation gets more complex, the treatment plan will become more complex—more forms of treatment and greater therapist range and flexibility will be required. The complexity in a therapy situation is related to several variables, including the number of therapeutic tasks that need to be accomplished, the client's readiness level (the less ready the client, the longer the developmental process until she completes the task), and the severity of the client's dysfunction. Karen and Debra exemplify but two points on the therapeutic continuum. As you reviewed their cases, we hope you could see how form and style figure into the treatment planning equation. Chapter Seven continues to address the issue of assessment for treatment planning using the ACT model.

7

⊞ ⊞ ⊞ ⊞ ⊞ ⊞ ⊞ ⊞ ⊞ ⊞ ⊞ ⊞ ⊞

Assessing Clients
and Developing
Effective Treatment Plans

Every time we sit across from a new client, we are faced with the same predicament. We are required to make an efficient and accurate clinical assessment of the client. Clinical assessment usually takes place for one of two reasons. Assessment either helps to facilitate a clinical decision or it helps the therapist obtain a picture of the client's current functioning. In either case, its purpose is to assist the therapist in developing a plan for treatment.

The assessment process involves many questions. Why is the client in treatment? What kind of person do we have here? What does the therapist need to know about the client? Can the therapist formulate a diagnostic impression of the client? What does the client think needs to happen in treatment? What does the counselor think needs to happen? What will be the best kind of treatment for this client? Who will be the best therapist for this person? These are not questions that can be taken lightly or that can always be answered easily. Without some skill at clinical assessment, the therapist is like the lost traveler who has no map to tell him where he is and where he is going. To assess a client appropriately is to pinpoint where we are. To identify what needs to happen in treatment tells us where we need to go. The treatment plan becomes the vehicle that takes therapy from here to there.

121

The ACT Model and Assessment

Therapeutic assessment is a process of evaluating all the relevant variables pertaining to the client and the client's treatment. In the ACT model, these are the relevant variables: What does the client need to accomplish? How ready is the client to work toward these goals? What does the therapist need to do to assist the client in meeting these goals? And how will treatment be monitored and evaluated?

Central to the ACT model is the belief that the therapist should behave differently along the dimensions of direction and support with different clients, with the same client at different points in time, and with the same client accomplishing different tasks. The critical point here is that the therapist's behavior varies systematically with the specific treatment goals. In order to know what style a therapist might best employ, the therapeutic tasks must be established. In order for the tasks to be established, the goals of treatment must be determined. In order for there to be treatment goals, the client's problems must be delineated. Therefore, the basic sequence of the assessment process involves:

- Assessment of the therapeutic problems or issues
- Decision on the goals of therapy
- Development of a treatment plan to meet these therapeutic goals
- A mechanism for assessing and monitoring the progress of treatment

The reader familiar with the DSM-III, who has filled out the treatment review form for insurance purposes, will readily recognize this four-step sequence. One of the benefits in using the ACT system as an aspect of case conceptualization is the ease with which that process can be communicated to others for review.

Assessing Therapeutic Problems

In the ACT model, assessment is more than the traditional blend of testing and interviewing in order to develop a specific diagnosis and treatment plan. But early in most therapy situations, it is essential for the therapist to gain an understanding of the client and the client's problems, to be able to make a differential diagnosis, and to develop a basic treatment plan. ACT does not offer a specific procedure for this aspect of assessment. Rather, it encourages the clinician to continue to use his or her interviewing and testing methods for gaining a working knowledge of the client. Our model does suggest, however, that the therapist's basic methods for assessing the client's therapeutic problems may need augmentation in order to select the best treatment approach for dealing with the various goals of therapy. This ongoing assessment component, which can help therapists to tailor treatment to the client's developmental level with respect to specific therapeutic goals, is the subject of the remainder of this chapter.

Determining the Goals of Treatment

By now, it should be clear that ACT visualizes therapy as a series of tasks to be accomplished. The assessment of what tasks need to be accomplished takes place through an ongoing, interactive process between client and therapist. Therapy tasks can be affective, cognitive, and behavioral. Although different therapists using different theoretical frameworks may conceptualize clinical problems differently, it is our contention that all therapies focus on the accomplishment of certain tasks. Perhaps the task is to establish a therapeutic environment in which the client feels free to talk. Perhaps the task is for the client to know herself better. Or perhaps the task is for the client to engage in specific new behavior. In any event, one major question is: Who sets the tasks? Is it the therapist? (The therapist tells the client that she needs to focus on drinking less.) Is it the client? (The client tells the therapist that she wants help in cutting down on drinking.) Is it a social agent? (The court tells the person who has received a DUI that she can either go to jail or submit to an alcohol treatment program.) Once a task has been established, the style of therapeutic intervention depends on the specific task to be accomplished and the client's competence, confidence, and motivation related to that task.

Content and Process in Psychotherapy. Before we discuss how a therapist clarifies the best-fitting treatment approach, two important distinctions need to be made. The first is between content and process in therapy. Content and process distinctions are well known to most therapists. The content of therapy relates to *what* gets attention whereas the process of therapy entails *how* therapy will evolve and proceed. The content of therapy varies widely from client to client. One client may be dealing with a marital relationship, another with long-standing depression, another with how to be a good parent, and yet another with interpersonal relationships at work.

Therapeutic process varies among clients as well. The focus on process attends to the interaction between therapist and client: who does what, when things happen, and how the therapy gets accomplished. Process tasks can be defined that cut across various content domains of therapy. The important point for ACT is that both content tasks and process tasks involve a systematic variance in therapist style that is determined by the task to be accomplished and the client's readiness. The following list presents a range of common therapy process tasks.

- Develop rapport
- Build trust

- Gain information
- Teach/learn a skill
- Gain insight
- Catharsis

- Uncover repressed material

- Build self-esteem
- Teach/learn a new coping mechanism
- Support new behavior
- Enhance transference
- Desensitization
- Confront denial/ avoidance
- Give emotional support

To illustrate how the therapist's style varies systematically with the client's readiness, we will consider the process task of gaining information from the client. How we go about gathering information depends on the client's readiness related to the task of giving information. How willing, able, and confident the client is to share information will influence how the therapist goes about getting it.

With a willing and able client (R4), the therapist may only need S4 behavior to gain information: "Tell me why you decided on counseling at this time." A less confident client (R3) might need more S3 behavior from the therapist. In S3 the information-gathering process is typified by empathic listening, open-ended questions, and sharing control of the process and the content with the client. The question would stay the same: "Can you tell me what made you decide on counseling at this time?" But recognizing the client's apprehension, the therapist would be very responsive to the client in order to create an accepting and comfortable therapeutic atmosphere. To gather information from a client who is unable but willing (R2), an S2 approach is indicated. The therapist would need to assist the client by providing more direction. Structured questions, closed questions, and questions that ask for specific information facilitate the process for the client who has difficulty sharing. It is easier for such a client to respond to specific questions—"Are you and your wife arguing about money issues?" "Isn't there enough money?" "Do you tend to disagree about how to spend money?"—than it would be for him to respond to "Tell me about your financial situation." When the client is unsure, the therapist must take primary control over the content and process of gathering information. If the client is both unable and unwilling to give relevant information (R1), the therapist may not only control the content and the process but will have to rely increasingly on other sources of information. Sources other than the client's verbal report are particularly important in S1 information gathering. Behavioral observation, social and family histories, and information gained from projective and objective personality testing may be more important sources of information than the client's verbal reports in these cases. If we only went by the verbal reports of unwilling and unable clients, we would believe that our prisons were filled with prisoners who "didn't do it" and that our inpatient alcohol units were filled with people who "don't have a drinking problem."

Sequential and Interactive Issues in Psychotherapy. A second distinction related to the therapeutic process is important for understanding assessment from the ACT perspective. Therapy can be viewed as a sequential process or as an interactive one. While much of the process of counseling and psychotherapy moves through a predictable sequence, therapy is also highly interactive. A therapist's theoretical orientation influences the information that he or she seeks during counseling and, conversely, information gained during therapy alters the clinician's conceptualization of the problem, the goals for treatment, and the therapeutic methods to be employed.

Since the ACT model appreciates the developmental aspects of both the client and the therapy process, it requires that assessment be interactive as well as sequential. There is nothing static about therapy. Over the entire course of treatment, new therapeutic tasks continue to develop. And at any point in the therapy process, clients may be working on a number of different tasks—tasks for which their readiness level may vary. Therapists, then, systematically use a variety of styles at any given time.

ACT predicts confusion for the client in therapy programs that view diagnosis and treatment sequentially. Diagnostic techniques consistent with low levels of readiness are frequently applied to clients in programs that emphasize evaluation for initial diagnosis. An S1 assessment procedure is highly structured and usually involves a standard battery for objective and projective instruments. It is not unusual for this S1 assessment to be followed by either S3 or S4 therapy. The sudden switch from a high-structure/low-support situation to a low-structure/high- or low-support treatment is inconsistent with the one-step-at-a-time principle that is basic to the ACT system. Moreover, when the professional involved in assessment and diagnosis is different from the professional involved in treatment, there is an even greater likelihood that the interactive characteristics of the process will not receive sufficient attention.

Developing a Treatment Plan

With content/process and sequential/interactive distinctions in mind, we can proceed to the assessment question related to providing the therapeutic roadmap. In order to determine which route is likely to move the client from where he is to where he wants to go, we must now turn our attention to task readiness—a key concept in the ACT model. What is the client's readiness level with respect to the therapeutic tasks he must perform? The concept of developmental readiness can be broken down into three elements:

- *Willingness:* How willing is the person to engage in the tasks that are necessary? How willing is the person to accept and work toward the goals of therapy?
- *Ability:* How competent is the person to engage in the necessary instrumental, cognitive, and affective behavior necessary to accomplish the task?
- *Confidence:* What is the individual's own assessment of his ability to perform the tasks? How secure does he feel about his ability to complete the tasks?

The client's readiness level influences the amount of direction and support provided by the therapist. ACT is aimed at finding the best match between the therapist's directive and supportive style and the client's readiness level. The goal is for the therapist to offer no more and no less direction and support than the client requires for a task. Then the therapist moves with the client, one step at a time, until the necessary direction and support pertaining to the therapeutic task eventually reside within the client and his or her environment. Once that occurs, the therapist's direction and support are no longer needed. Therapy can then be terminated appropriately.

Direction and Support in Therapy. This is a good time to review the role of direction and support in the ACT model. In the ACT model, the direction dimension is concerned with who provides how much direction or structure in the therapy situation. What will be done? How will it be done? When will it be done? Who will do what? Under what circumstances? All these questions must be answered before a task can be accomplished. In S1, the therapist provides most of the direction. It is the therapist who determines what will happen in a specific therapeutic task, when it will happen, and how it will happen. Suppose we have a client who must learn to feel and express her anger in an appropriate manner. And suppose that client not only has great difficulty in feeling and expressing her anger but is also reluctant to do so. With such a goal and a somewhat unwilling and unable client, an S1 approach would be the treatment of choice according to ACT. Using an S1 or S2 high-direction approach, a specific hostility release program might be established. Twice a week, the therapist and the client would retreat to an environment that was designated "safe" for hostility release. The client would be instructed to think about a situation that detonated her anger. If she were unable to think of such a situation, the therapist might assist her by recounting something that previously induced anger in her. In the early phases of such a program, it might be sufficient that the client just remember and feel her anger. Later she might be given a plastic bat or a bataka and be told to hit a large pillow with it. Or there might be a punching bag. Similarly the client might be prompted to yell and scream the appropriate angry responses. In any case, the treatment is highly structured by the therapist. The hostility release program tells the client where, when, and how to accomplish the task.

The same task, to feel and express anger, might also be deemed the treatment of choice for another client—a client who easily experiences angry feelings and has no trouble articulating them. But this second client would be at a much higher readiness level because he or she is willing and able to participate in the task. In this case a structured hostility release program would not be necessary. An S3 or S4 low-direction approach would be more appropriate. All that the client might need from the therapist is permission to express his or her anger during the therapy hour. How he or she expresses the anger and what the anger focuses on would be left to the client.

Support is the second dimension of therapy. This dimension centers on the client experiencing a sense of caring, concern, approval, praise, reinforcement, or feedback from the therapist. As with direction, the amount of support that the therapist needs to provide with respect to a task may vary from very little to very much. Using anger release as an example again, we think you can see that the unwilling and unable client is going to require a lot of positive reinforcement in order to make progress. Progress may need to be measured in very small increments and the reinforcement meted out accordingly: "That was excellent. You really seemed to be remembering your upset with your daughter. I hope it felt good to talk about it, even if it was a little scary." While this kind of support would be appropriate for the person inexperienced at expressing anger, it would be preposterous to offer such support to a client who has always been able to articulate angry feelings. To commend a four-year-old for tying his shoes is one thing. To commend a fourteen-year-old for the same behavior is another.

Assessing Direction for Treatment Planning. A pertinent question for treatment planning is the *source* of the direction. The therapist needs information about potential sources of direction for the client. The following paragraphs indicate the kinds of questions the therapist needs to answer before the best treatment approach can be initiated. We have grouped the questions by area of focus. Clearly, these questions are only intended to exemplify the kinds of questions that will help the therapist evaluate the client's readiness and determine how much direction or structure the therapist needs to provide. The list is not exhaustive. Nor would all of these questions be necessary for one client tackling one therapeutic task.

One source of direction is *experience*. The therapist wants to assess the client's experience level related to the specific task to be tackled. The client's past experience (or lack of it) regarding a therapeutic task often gives the therapist information about ability, as well as clues as to why a client may be more or less willing to approach a certain task. Past experience related to both the content and the process of the task can be a source of direction for the client. Some issues to be assessed vis-à-vis the client's experience level include the following questions.

Has the person ever performed this task before? If so, what were the results? The more successful past experience the client has had, the more these past experiences themselves can provide current structure for the client. The therapist will need to structure the task of expressing anger for the client who has never expressed it before. The client who expressed anger several times as a child and was harshly beaten in retaliation is certainly going to be less willing, and therefore more reliant on direction, than the client who expresses anger readily and has not suffered any dire consequences for doing so. If successful past experience has been minimal, the therapist will have to supply more direction.

Does the person have experience or skills that can be transferred to learning the present task? Skills that are similar to a new skill to be learned also provide direction for the client. If our hypothetical client has been able to feel and express other, more positive feelings easily, he may be able to draw on that experience as the new task is undertaken. The more transferable skills the client possesses related to the therapeutic task, the less the need for a highly structured therapy situation.

What skills and experiences does the person have that can form the basis for learning the present task? If the client has been a quick learner in other situations, his confidence will be high. Thus the client will be more ready and less in need of external direction for accomplishment of the task. Or perhaps the client is skilled at imagining how other people might behave if they were angry and can use fantasy to prompt his own responses. The more skills and experiences available to the client, the less structure the therapist will need to apply.

If the client has had little experience at this task or a related one, what accounts for the lack of experience? A lack of exposure? A lack of willingness? Avoidance? The kind of direction a therapist will need to use depends on pinpointing the roots of the low readiness level. A therapist might suggest movies depicting anger scenes to the client who has had no exposure to appropriate role models. But if the client is avoiding anger because of anxiety, the therapist's direction might focus on the client's cognitive messages to himself.

We turn now to *significant environmental sources.* Direction for the client working on new tasks can come from sources other than the client or the therapist. Other individuals, groups, and activities can provide the structure necessary to the successful completion of a therapeutic task.

What are the family subcultural and cultural norms related to the task? Are there others in the client's environment who can model the new behavior the client is trying to learn? If these norms do not assist in structuring the client's growth around the task, therapy must provide more direction. For example, if the significant others in the client's environment do not know how (or do not want) to help the client achieve his goals, then the structure for helping the client with the task will have to be provided by the therapy situation.

How have the client's role models performed? Good role models are a source of direction for the client. If there are few or none, direction needs to be supplied within the context of therapy.

What significant sources of direction exist in the community, in printed material, or in the media? Some sources of direction for the client learning a new task are rooted in activities. Perhaps there are anger management workshops or self-help books to which the client can be directed. There may be movies or plays showing the behavior that the client is trying to master. You can see that these adjuncts to therapy can provide direction. If they are used, the therapist can cut back on the direction component within the therapy setting.

How aware is the client of these resources? If the client brings us information about an anger management workshop, he is providing his own direction. If the therapist needs to inform the client about the workshop, then the therapist is taking responsibility for the direction. The more aware the client is of other resources, the less direction the therapist needs to provide for making him aware.

How likely is the client to be able and willing to use these sources of direction? The less able and willing the client is, of course, the more directive the therapist needs to be. Therapists must be realistic about the structure they provide. A client with little money and no transportation is unlikely to attend a six-week anger management course and therefore unlikely to be successful with such a directive. The therapist will have to transfer the structure of the anger management course into the therapy setting.

What are the external sources of structure on the client's time, energy, and attention? The client who is seeking improved communication with his or her spouse but whose schedule makes marital communication impossible will need therapeutic direction about the use of time and energy. A source of structure is present for the client who has already built in some daily time with his or her spouse.

Our next focus is on *internal client direction*. The client can provide varying amounts of direction for himself or herself. How able has the client been in learning new tasks? Strange as it may seem, success at learning to play tennis can provide the client with some direction about success at learning to express anger. People who have mastered other skills understand better the skill-building process.

How willing is the client to accomplish the task? The greater the client's willingness to participate in the treatment process, the more ready he is to learn and the less directive the therapist and other sources of structure need to be. If the client really wants to be more proficient at expressing hostility, the therapist will need fewer carrots and sticks. Willingness is a great source of internal direction for the client.

How confident is the client in this area of his life? The client's internal direction increases in proportion to his belief that success is possible. He is more likely to try letting a friend know that he is angry with him if he believes that the interaction is likely to go well. If he thinks failure is imminent, he will need an external push toward task accomplishment.

How central is the task to the client's sense of integrity and identity? Clients will obviously invest more of themselves in tasks they view as important than in those that seem minor and peripheral. The client who says, "If I can't learn to let people know when I am angry with them, then I am a wimp," is more likely to direct himself to practice the new behavior than the client who says, "Being able to express anger doesn't say anything much about me." Clients who view the therapeutic task as integral to their sense of self are likely to provide their own direction.

What are the internal barriers to task accomplishment? Does the client talk to himself in a way that provides direction? "I will feel some relief once I can get these pent-up angry feelings out." Or will it take some outside direction to compensate for or change a habit that is a barrier to task accomplishment? The client says, "If I express anger, people won't like me anymore." The therapist may need to be directive and say, "I want you to talk to yourself in a new way. Say to yourself, 'If I express anger, people may be surprised and uncomfortable but they won't stop liking me.'"

How does this task relate to the client's defenses and coping methods? The client who feels threatened by the therapeutic task is going to need more external direction than the client who does not believe that the new behavior will seriously affect the situation or the sense of self. A client is unlikely to provide self-direction for new processes that are threatening.

Once a therapist has assessed the client's sources of direction for the accomplishment of a therapeutic task, attention can focus on providing direction in treatment planning. The answers to the following questions help the therapist find the best-fitting style with regard to direction.

Given the preceding assessment, how much and what kinds of direction are necessary? The therapist will be systematically matching the amount of direction provided in therapy to the client's need for direction, and that need will be determined by assessing how much direction is provided elsewhere—through the client's past experience, through other people in the client's environment, and through the client's own strengths.

Is it possible to provide the necessary direction? If not, what can be done? Each of us must make that decision based on our clinical skills, the treatment setting within which we work, and the needs of the client. Referral is sometimes the best answer. Or we may suggest some kind of augmentation to our treatment plan. For example, analysts screen their patients. As stated earlier, ACT suggests that if analysis cannot provide sufficient direction, then the person is not a good candidate for analysis. Such clients are often referred for other treatment. The setting of the treatment process is equally important. If the therapist works in an individual, outpatient setting and the client needs the structure of an inpatient situation, then the therapist is not able to provide the necessary structure.

Does the assessment thus far suggest the need to reassess therapeutic goals and tasks? If there is no way at the present time for the client to receive sufficient direction for the task, the task may need to be postponed until other tasks are accomplished or until sufficient direction can be established. One of our clients had repressed her anger so long that she was frightened about how it might get expressed. The expression of her anger was a goal, but working on that goal was postponed until she could arrange to take off from work for several weeks in order to work on that task as an inpatient and learn ways of expressing anger.

What are the appropriate intervals for monitoring task accomplishment? Since treatment is not a static process, the therapist will be varying direction based on the client's readiness level. Over the course of treatment, it is assumed that the client is becoming more ready with regard to the task being worked on. Therefore, as therapy progresses the therapist will be offering less and less direction. Periodic reassessment is in order.

Signs of a Mismatch on Direction. A mismatch between the therapist and the client with respect to direction can impede treatment. Sometimes the therapist provides more direction than is necessary, sometimes less. While at times a directional mismatch can be difficult to detect, for the most part there are clear indicators of too much or too little direction. The following discussion gives several clinical examples of various mismatches on the direction component and lists the signs which suggest a therapist/client mismatch.

Sometimes the therapist gives *more* direction than the client needs. Clinical examples of overdirection in treatment abound. For example, whenever therapy is not terminated appropriately and the client is kept in treatment longer than necessary, too much direction is being provided. As we mentioned earlier, institutional settings and some programmatic settings often provide too much direction in the sense that they do not take their clients through a developmental sequence. Therapists can make the same mistake. Unnecessary hospitalization can be the result of overdirection. We see this when someone expressing depression is immediately hospitalized or when parents discover some marijuana in their adolescent's room and proceed to rush him to an adolescent psychiatric unit. Such cases more likely represent crises for people other than the identified patient. Premature problem solving is another form of overdirection. Therapists who too quickly suggest "Quit your job!" or "Get a divorce" are obviously overdirective. Intentional overdirection is called paradox. Properly executed paradoxical interventions are intentional mismatches that are so obvious that the client resists them. While paradox can be a useful intervention for fighting resistance, it is often, unfortunately, used inappropriately and unskillfully. The following list presents some specific signs of overdirection in treatment:

- *Dismissing or discounting the client's input:* Suppose the therapist is trying to persuade a client to use a plastic baseball bat in order to release angry feelings while the client is suggesting that he might be able to get rid of some of his angry feelings by bowling and imagining that the head pin is his boss. You can see in this example that the client can clearly provide more of his own direction than the therapist is allowing.
- *Arguments between therapist and client over exact means to an end:*

Client:	I've been thinking about how hard it is for me to express my anger. I read that the Med School is offering an assertiveness class and I think I'm going to take it. *[Client is providing own direction.]*
Therapist:	I think we need to talk some about this. I'm concerned that a group setting might not be the best place to work on this. *[Therapist is reluctant to let client self-direct.]*
Client:	I guess part of my reason for wanting to go to the class is that I feel I might learn some ways to express myself better. *[Client continues to try to provide direction.]*

> *Therapist:*   Let's talk about the things that are
>   blocking you. *[Control battle continues.]*
> *Client:*   I think I'm tired of talking. I want to
>   find a way to express myself better and
>   the class sounds like a good idea. *[Client
>   continues to express awareness of the mis-
>   match.]*

- *Nominal compliance by the client without internalization or transfer to similar situations:* Like the overdirected adolescent who does the minimum necessary to avoid punishment, the overdirected client goes through the motions of what is expected of him or her without enthusiasm and without really internalizing the new behavior or feelings. Giving more direction than is needed is infantilizing.
- *Passive-aggressive behavior on the part of the client:* Such behavior may indicate a control struggle. Passive-aggressive control battles are much less open than the argument described above. The client who shows up late for appointments, fails to do assignments, or sabotages progress may be reacting to more therapist direction than is necessary.
- *Reduced motivation and effort directed toward the task:* Giving more direction than the client needs results in a regressive cycle. Rather than becoming more motivated, more competent, and more confident, the client becomes less so. The once conscientious client becomes more sporadic in attendance, shows less follow-through on assignments, or backslides on the therapeutic task itself

Treatment that provides *less* direction than the client needs can be as problematic as treatment that provides too much direction. Such mismatches have been seen in most of our practices at one time or another. There is the overwhelmed and struggling mother of six who is asking for concrete suggestions for managing her life but is being requested to get in touch with her feelings instead. Premature terminations exemplify less direction than needed. A common form of therapist confusion is related to the subtle difference between an S2 and an S3 stance. The early training focus on being a listener and empathizer rather than an advice giver may result in a therapist who is afraid to offer specific suggestions in outpatient therapy. Yet sometimes that is exactly what the client needs. Being able to match the client on direction involves being able to shift back and forth between an S2 and an S3 style depending on the therapeutic task. The following list presents some specific signs of underdirection in treatment:

- *Client questions about direction, purpose, and role:* John had been in therapy for three years before deciding to find another therapist. He reported that he never could figure out exactly what his previous therapy had been about. He expressed frustration about unsuccessfully trying to get the therapist to give him some feedback and help him understand things that were problematic in his life. He had many questions about direction, purpose, and role that the therapist was not reading as John's lack of competence and confidence. The new therapist had more range and was able to be more directive. Six sessions later, John had made significant progress and his confidence had grown to the point where he was asking for much less direction.
- *Extreme anxiety in the client:* Since ambiguity often results in greater anxiety, it is important to ask ourselves if the client needs more specific structure when we observe heightened anxiety. "Work on expressing your anger this week" is too vague and therefore too anxiety-provoking for many clients. They simply do not know how to do that. It is better to request, "I want you to be aware of any feelings of irritation you experience this week. In fact, keep a notepad handy and jot down a few notes to yourself about what irritated you."
- *Random attempts to produce structure:* The directive dimension in therapy involves a systematic plan for moving the client through a sequential process in which externalized structure moves to internalized direction. Random attempts by the therapist to provide structure indicate that more direction is needed but the treatment plan has not been well constructed.

- *Appeals to other sources for direction:* Frequent referrals to structured groups or a heavy reliance on hospitalization may be
  red flags that insufficient direction is being provided in
  therapy itself. It is perfectly acceptable and often essential
  for a therapist to give assignments and make requests about
  a client's behavior. "I have two requests to make of you.
  I want you to let me know when you are angry with me about
  something, and I want you to practice at least once this week
  telling your husband when something irritates you." Such
  a request may be a more appropriate use of direction than
  sending the client to an assertiveness class.
- *Drifting out of therapy:* Clients who drift out of therapy may
  be sending a message that they did not find sufficient direction in the therapy situation. Sporadic attendance may be
  the first sign of drifting out of therapy.

Assessing Support for Treatment Planning. The analysis of a
client's support system enables the ACT therapist to reinforce,
strengthen, and encourage the use of sources of support other
than therapy. Such an analysis may also result in the identifica-
tion of problems, goals, and tasks germane to the development
and expansion of the client's support system. A client's support system can be analyzed by assessing the following categories:
internal support, social support, environmental support, and
the therapeutic task itself.

The basic question regarding *internal support* involves how
capable the client is of providing himself or herself with support, reinforcement, feedback, praise, and encouragement.
Again, the goal of successful therapy is for the client to develop
sufficient sources of support to permit therapy to terminate
without significant loss to the client. A sure sign of a client's
being ready to terminate therapy is when he forgets appointments because other activities interfere with his appointment
time.

Social support focuses on the person's social network. Note
here that the assessment considers both the extent of the social
network and the degree of supportiveness related to the therapeutic tasks. An understanding of systems theory and social net-

work concepts is helpful in this aspect of the assessment. The following questions should be entertained in order to appreciate the amount of social support a client receives.

What is the nature of the family relationship? In what ways are persons in the family likely to support the client's therapeutic progress?

What social systems other than the family are significant for the client? Work groups? Organized social groups? Church groups? Friends?

How, who, and to what degree are the major roles filled for the client? These major roles include:

- *Confronter:* Gives the client feedback about off-target or self-defeating behavior.
- *Nurturer:* Supports and "takes care" of the client. Provides the client's unconditional positive regard.
- *Admirer:* By whom and in what contexts is the client admired?
- *Confidant:* In whom can the client confide with a sense of trust?
- *Dependent:* In what contexts is the client depended upon by others? By whom? Does the client have a spouse, children, or friends for whom he feels indispensable?

What changes in the client's social network are likely to result from the client's therapeutic changes? If the client makes significant changes, will he lose support in some places and gain support in others? Where? How much? For example, the client who gets better at expressing anger may not experience much support for that behavior from family members and friends. The therapist may need to strengthen the client's internal support for that behavior to compensate for the external support he once received for the lack of angry expression.

What roles need to be filled temporarily by therapeutic intervention? The therapist is assessing how he or she can provide temporary support while working with the client to develop those sources in places other than therapy.

Assessment of environmental and circumstantial support includes answers to questions like these:

- What are the client's financial resources?
- What community resources are available to the client?
- What legal supports exist for the client?
- What primary or adjunctive treatment options are available to the client?

Finally, support can result from the *therapeutic task* itself. The therapist assesses:

- To what extent does the task itself provide feedback and reinforcement to the client?
- What is the typical learning curve for the task? Is this the kind of task where initial efforts are likely to produce positive results? Is it likely that initial efforts at change will result in less positive outcomes for a period of time?

Assessing the Therapist for Treatment Planning. Up to this point in the chapter, assessment has concerned the therapeutic tasks the client needs to accomplish and the client's readiness to undertake these tasks. Assessment, however, includes a third element that relates to the therapist. Clearly, each therapist has a responsibility to determine his or her own willingness, ability, and confidence to provide the appropriate amount of direction and support to match the client's needs. If this self-assessment suggests that the therapist is a mismatch for the client, the therapist has several options: to work at increasing his or her style range and flexibility, to limit his or her practice, to practice less than optimal therapy, or to develop good referral resources in adjunctive areas.

In addition to assessing one's own readiness level for providing therapy to a client, the therapist needs to examine the source of his or her power for the relationship with the client. The notion of therapist power relates directly to the concept of leadership power. Leadership is the ability to influence another person, and power addresses the reason the follower agrees to be led. In equating therapists with leaders, we are arguing that therapy is also the ability to influence another person and that there are power issues related to therapy that address the reasons a client would agree to the therapy.

The variety of reasons for following a leader have been categorized by French and Raven (1959). Their seven categories represent the various power bases from which a person may attempt to influence or lead. The bases identified by French and Raven are as relevant to treatment professionals as to supervisors and managers. In discussing each power base and its relationship to therapy, we will cite relevant treatment examples. Your own direct and observational experiences also will enrich your understanding of the importance of power bases in therapy.

Coercive power is the power to administer sanctions or punishment. This power base has all the characteristics associated with negative reinforcers. The therapist should be especially mindful of the following characteristics:

- Few events are inherently punishing for all people. Jail, death, or starvation may "hold no sting" for some people; if not, the coercive power of the event is reduced.
- Punishment can be effective for stopping certain behavior. It appears to be less effective, however, for learning new behavior.
- Coercion can gain compliance, but once the coercive threat is removed the compliance often stops.
- Coercion is best used as a recognized deterrent force that remains undelivered.

Some years ago, one of the authors had a client whose problem related to her always being late. Because of her chronic tardiness, other people, especially her employer, regarded her as irresponsible. Predictably, she was always late for therapy appointments as well. Before the therapist had established a meaningful relationship with the client, there was little opportunity to be coercive about her lateness. The therapist had no "stick." However, once the therapist became important to the client and once the client viewed the therapy hour as desirable, the therapist was able to announce: "One of the ways we are going to work on your lateness problem is to start right here in therapy. I expect you to be on time. Any appointment for which you are more than five minutes late, I will cancel for the week." Several times appointments were canceled by the therapist but, as anticipated, the client's behavior started to turn in the appropriate direction. Eventually, the timeliness in therapy was transferred to other situations.

Sometimes coercive power gets people into treatment because treatment is seen as the lesser of two evils: treatment or you lose your family; treatment or you go to jail. The initial coercive power gets the client into treatment. But if the coercive threat remains the major reason for being there, the treatment is unlikely to be effective.

Coercive power is based on fear. But some fearful clients are not in treatment because of coercion but because they are looking for expert help. These clients initially seek treatment out of fear of what will happen to them if they do not change. This fear is often expressed in statements like the following: "If I don't do something about this now, I'm afraid I'll . . . " Whether the fear is the loss of a job, loss of life, or loss of wife, the client is being motivated to seek treatment out of fear of some sort of negative sanction. However, the therapist's power really emanates from the client's perception of the therapist as an expert who can be helpful. This power would become coercive only if the client believed that the therapist could affect the loss of job or wife.

Connective power is gained by association with other powerful individuals, groups, and institutions. It is power by association. Unless the connection is to a power base relevant to the client, it will not be influential. A therapist friend of ours, who was also influential in local politics, was sometimes sought out for therapy by clients impressed by his political clout—a case of connective power. Each of the authors is married to a therapist, and sometimes our services are requested as a result of our spouses' reputation. All therapists who publicize their association with a particular accrediting group are making use of connective power. "I am a licensed psychologist." "I am a licensed clinical social worker." "I belong to a national association of marital and family therapists." Each of these affiliations is a form of connective power. As therapists, each of us chooses to emphasize or downplay certain associations in order to enhance our connective power. Much of traditional rapport building is establishing common connections with a client—emphasizing certain aspects of your experience, background, and personality in order to reduce the connections you wish to deemphasize and increase the connections you consider most helpful.

Expert power is based on the perceived expertise of the therapist or the therapy setting. "Why are you doing that?" "Because Dr. Murphy told me to, and she should know!" This expert power base is often associated with credentials, known experience, position power, and connective power. Most clients seeking professional services are seeking expert power. Frequently, this power base continues to develop over the course of treatment as the therapist's credibility, based on the client's experience, increases. If the treatment plan calls for much S1 and S2 behavior by the therapist, the expert power base is critical. The more directive and intrusive the treatment, the more perceived expertise is needed. Clients must believe in the therapist's prescriptive abilities. Marianne Walters, a noted family therapist, makes a point of cautioning audiences against going out and using high-risk techniques unless they have the expertise to do so. Would that other "masters of the craft" offered similar cautions to novice therapists. It is fitting that most training in the helping professions initially centers on S3 behaviors of listening and clarifying. A therapist does not need a lot of expertise in order to listen, clarify, and support.

Position power resides in the role ascribed to the therapist. It is closely tied to authority issues. "Do what I tell you!" "Why?" "Because I'm your . . . " Whether that role is parent, boss, minister, therapist, or doctor, the person making such a statement has the power associated with that statement only while in that position. *Any* social worker may have the power to determine a client's eligibility for a particular program. In such cases, the power is related to the position, not to the attributes of one particular social worker. Since the position of therapist is not inherently powerful, the therapist must often establish expert power in order to give weight to the therapy process. In assessing their position power, therapists need to be asking what resources, just by virtue of position, are at their disposal. Can they recommend parole, child custody, program eligibility, or the like? If this power base is weak, and it often is, other power bases must be established.

Information power involves having access to relevant and important information. To some extent the less easily obtained the information, the more important this power base becomes. Frequently, as a professional in a community you have access to information on what resources exist, the quality of a program, and whom to contact for an expeditious referral. ''I can't help you, but I know someone who can.'' A good referral combines information power with expert and connective power, since your professional judgment and expertise in evaluating the information are also involved. Initially in many therapy relationships the client has a wealth of information relevant to the problem and treatment, whereas the therapist has very little information power because of his or her lack of knowledge of the client. As the client shares information and the therapist shares expertise, the power base begins to equalize. Eventually the therapist may have more information power than the client.

Personal power is based on the therapist's qualities. Whereas coercive power is rooted in fear and expert power in respect, personal power is rooted in affection. ''I'll do that because I like you.'' ''I wouldn't do this for anyone else, but since it's you . . . '' The therapist's personal power base frequently increases during the course of therapy as the therapist becomes increasingly significant to the client. Similarly, the therapist may well develop increasing empathy, liking, and investment in the client, thereby giving the client a personal power base with the therapist. It may be easier for some of our clients than for others to reschedule an appointment, for example. Whether we call it transference and countertransference or the therapeutic alliance, this base is critical for the full range of ACT styles to be effective.

Reward power emanates from the therapist's ability to control relevant rewards for the client. Reward power operates consistently with the principles of reinforcement. Certain principles are particularly important in the progressive cycle of the ACT system:

- Few things, if any, are inherently rewarding. To be a reward, something must be relevant and important to the person being rewarded. Money, time off, feeling less depressed, or being more attractive may or may not be rewarding to a person.

- Rewards shift from external, tangible, and immediate to internal, symbolic, and capable of delayed gratification as a client becomes more ready for a task and the therapist progresses from S1 through S4 styles.
- In the learning process small immediate reinforcements or corrections are generally more effective than one large reward after the goal is achieved. Shaping principles, in which behavior increasingly closer to the goal is rewarded, are important.
- The most powerful rewards for many clients become the approval and reinforcement of the therapist. This source of reinforcement is particularly important during parts of the learning process where effort does not produce results that are reinforced in the environment. When a client's initial attempts at assertiveness are greeted with angry outbursts from her spouse, for example, the therapist's support may be very important in maintaining and shaping the desired assertive behavior.

A therapist may use varying degrees of power from all the various power bases we have discussed. Any and all of the power bases may be used in each of the treatment styles. But some of the therapist power bases are more intrinsic to certain styles than others. The power bases most likely to be used in each treatment style are presented in Figure 7.

Inspection of Figure 7 shows several patterns. We begin with the pattern for style 1. To be effective with unwilling clients the therapist needs both a stick and a carrot. Expert power is needed, as well, because the therapist is making decisions about what needs to happen without much involvement from the client. If you are going to direct someone's treatment, you had better know what you are doing. Connective power and position power in S1 are frequently linked to broadening the extent of the power to reward and punish. For example, the court-referred client asks, "Do I have to come to treatment?" The therapist who

Figure 7. Relationship of Style and Power.

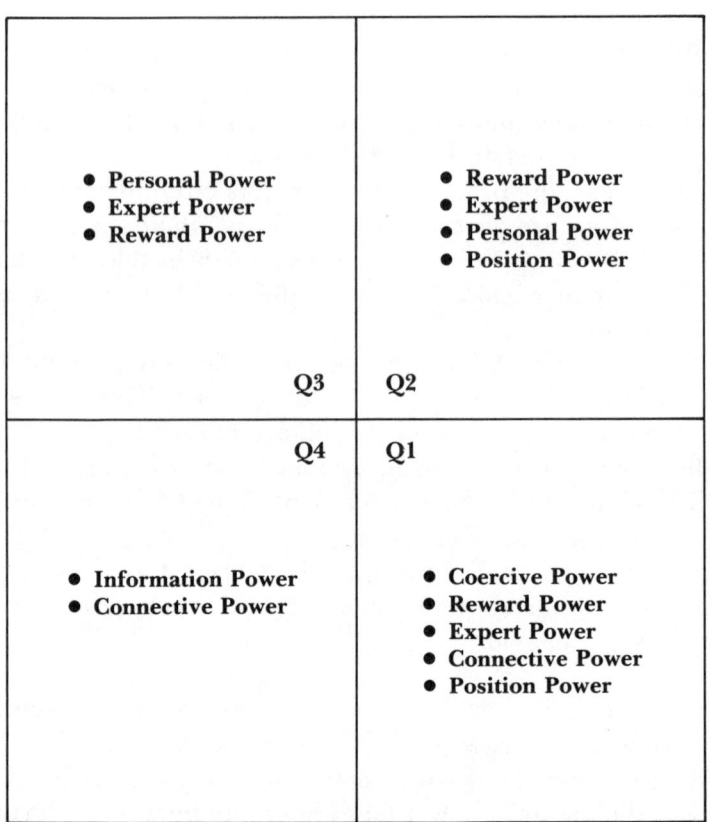

works closely with the judicial system is able to respond, ''Yes, you do have to come to treatment unless you want the court to reconsider its decision to send you to treatment rather than to prison.''

In style 2 the client is participating more fully in the treatment process, although most treatment decisions continue to be made by the therapist. This requires expert power. There is less reliance on coercive power but a continuing use of reward power, since positive reinforcement is an integral part of the learning process which is so active in S2. The S2 client is willing but unable and thus more attentive to the therapeutic relationship—that is, to personal power.

In style 3 personal power becomes very important while the other power bases diminish somewhat in importance. The therapist's support is the main component of reward power. Some expertness may still be required.

Finally, in style 4 information power and connective power are important in providing links to other sources of direction and support as the client makes the transition out of therapy.

In most outpatient psychotherapy, the therapist, intentionally or not, works to develop relationship and expert power. In situations where the therapist begins treatment having little position power or extrinsic coercive or reward power, he or she must begin with S3, moving through S2 to S1 only after the relationship has been established. This sequence of therapist styles is required in order for the therapist to gain the power base necessary to persuade the client to progress through the stages of treatment.

Monitoring the Treatment

The final step in the treatment planning process is the development of a method for monitoring therapy. How will the therapist and the client know how treatment is progressing? In keeping with the ACT model, there is no single method for evaluating treatment. Rather, the method of monitoring progress depends on the client's goals and the style of treatment.

Monitoring progress related to S1 goals requires an S1 monitoring method. Evaluation is external and does not rely on the client's self-report. With S1 goals and S1 treatment, the monitoring remains in the hands of the therapist. It is the therapist's observations that are applied to assessing progress. In addition to the therapist's observations, external criteria may be used. The anorexic client whose goal is not to lose any weight is weighed in order to see if the goal is being met. The incestuous father who is mandated to attend a group treatment program is evaluated through attendance and participation records. The substance abuser whose goal is to stay clean is monitored through blood tests and urinalysis. If treatment is progressing and the client is meeting goals, treatment goals eventually will become S2, S3, and S4 goals.

Monitoring of S2 treatment goals involves starting to teach the newly able client how to be involved in his or her own evaluation. The monitoring now becomes an interactive enterprise. The therapist is teaching the client how to observe his or her own progress. The anorexic adolescent who has maintained her weight for a number of weeks may now be working on a new goal of asserting herself with her parents. The therapist has asked her to keep a record of all the times she wanted to speak up about something and to bring that record to the therapy session. In the session, the therapist focuses on the kinds of incidents around which she was or was not able to assert herself and her feelings when she did or did not assert herself. The therapist continues to work with the client on new assertive behavior while helping her to monitor her progress.

As the client becomes more able and more confident about being assertive, treatment moves into an S3 mode, as does monitoring. The client is becoming capable of checking her own performance. In therapy she reports how well she handled a situation with her mother, and the therapist is congratulatory. With S3 goals and in S3 treatment, the therapist may be asking the client to recount progress. "Do you remember when that behavior was really difficult for you? It must feel great to look back and see what a long way you have come." Monitoring in the S2 and S3 modes is an interactive process involving both the client and the therapist.

Once treatment goals have been delegated fully to the client, the monitoring of progress is delegated as well. The previously anorexic, unassertive adolescent, who has conquered her eating problem and mastered speaking up for herself, no longer relies on an external monitoring method for those goals. She may now be working on several new goals. Depending on the style of the new goals and the treatment plan, monitoring will fall into one of the four ACT quadrants. In the therapy hour, this client still may occasionally self-evaluate her anorexia. "I'm feeling great about my eating habits. I think I really have this thing under control now."

If progress in treatment moves into a regressive cycle, the treatment plan moves back one step at a time, as does the monitoring process. If our previously anorexic client now says that she is beginning to notice that she is eating less, treatment falls back into an S3 style. The therapist offers support and suggests that the client go back to more careful self-monitoring. This one-step-at-a-time forward or backward movement continues, depending on whether the client is progressing or regressing. It is conceivable that if progress continued to regress significantly, the therapist might begin weighing the client again and going through the entire treatment process all over.

Process goals do not lend themselves very well to explicit evaluation. Such goals are more subjectively evaluated through observation and reflection. If the therapeutic task is for the client to develop trust in the therapist and in the therapy process, most of us would not prescribe trust exercises and then keep a checklist for exercises completed. Monitoring of that task, however, might be in any of the monitoring quadrants, depending on the client's readiness for that task. If the client is very distrustful, monitoring the early phases of that process would rest entirely with the therapist's observation and evaluation. The therapist would be noting signs of comfort and discomfort, looking for progress, and looking for those things to which the client seemed to respond in a more relaxed manner. A somewhat more ready client might be instructed, "Let me know if I ask any questions which feel intrusive." And still another client might be asked in a reminding way, "It seems you are feeling pretty comfortable with me lately and the process of therapy is no longer a mystery. Is that so?" And finally, the client for whom trust is no longer an issue at all has full responsibility for monitoring that task. The only time the therapist might expect to hear about it would be if a trust issue developed.

The purpose of monitoring the treatment process is to be able to continually reassess the client's readiness for specific therapeutic tasks. Since ACT defines treatment as a fluid process that takes the client from a less ready state to a more ready state and since the therapist's treatment plan and style must change as the client develops, this monitoring is an essential part of the therapy process. It is precisely this monitoring of the client's readiness level and development that tells the therapist how much direction and support to provide at various points in the treatment.

This chapter has focused on assessment and treatment planning using the ACT model. Assessing the client's therapeutic issues and deciding on the goals of treatment show us where we are and where we want to go. The treatment plan is the transportation that can then move the client from here to there. Evaluation involves checking the roadmap to be sure we are moving in the right direction. In Chapter Eight, we will be reviewing several cases to demonstrate the application of the ACT model to clinical work, both within the clinical hour and over the course of treatment.

8

🔳 🔳 🔳 🔳 🔳 🔳 🔳 🔳 🔳 🔳 🔳 🔳

Applying ACT over the Course of Treatment: Case Studies

ACT is a model for clinical practice—an applied rather than a theoretical model. Since all the basic principles of ACT have been introduced, it is critical at this point to demonstrate its practical application so that the reader can fully understand how to translate our description of the model into clinical practice. The best way to explain the application of ACT is through case material. In this chapter we will be using several cases to demonstrate the value and practicality of ACT for everyday clinical use.

As we sorted through the myriad cases with which we were personally familiar—not only from our own clinical caseloads but from the caseloads of our co-workers—we finally decided to describe three cases. Each was selected to illustrate certain facets of the process of using ACT to make targeted eclectic choices about treatment. A major goal of this chapter is to demonstrate the application of ACT over the course of the treatment process. To that end we will present a case from beginning to end, describing ACT's relationship to the long-term treatment plan as well as its application in the various therapy sessions.

The Client Who Improved Rapidly

Rachel was seen in therapy only nine times. And the therapeutic outcome was excellent. In many ways, Rachel represents a typical client who is seen in voluntary outpatient psychotherapy. She was bright, articulate, and bent on self-improvement. But in other ways she was different from many clients we see in this kind of setting. Rachel was not introspective, had little interest in psychology, and believed that life's problems always had pragmatic solutions. At the time of counseling, Rachel was thirty-five years old. She owned her own home and lived alone. A previous, childless marriage had ended in divorce about ten years earlier. Rachel worked in a government job at a managerial level. She held a master's degree in government from a well-respected university and would have described herself as a hardworking, upwardly mobile professional. The presenting concern, and the reason for seeking therapy, was depression. There was no past psychiatric or therapeutic history. For several months, Rachel had found herself suddenly crying for "no reason." On several occasions, she had even burst into tears at work. This was most unusual behavior for her as she had learned early not to cry and obeyed that admonition. Rachel did have complaints about both her professional and her personal life. She described her job as highly stressful. She disliked the work she was doing and the people with whom she was doing it. She desperately wanted to find another job.

Stress related to a significant love relationship was adding to her dismay. For the past year and a half, she had been involved with a married man and was beginning to find that situation untenable. Rachel had been referred to Terri, the therapist, by several mutual friends who respected Terri's clinical skills. Terri and Rachel had also worked together briefly on a charity project several years earlier. At that time, Rachel had liked Terri and found her friendly and competent.

Assessing Problems and Determining Treatment Goals. As we discussed in Chapter Seven, the initial therapeutic process involves assessing the therapeutic problems and determining the goals of treatment. With that in mind, the therapist set two treatment goals:

- Gather information about Rachel for purposes of assessment and treatment planning (content goal).
- Build a therapeutic relationship with the client (process goal).

Overall, Rachel was a highly motivated client. Because she was bright and verbal, but because she was not psychologically sophisticated and introspective, her ability level was mixed. Rachel's previous knowledge of the therapist and the high recommendations Terri had received from Rachel's friends suggested that Terri's power would emanate from personal and expert bases. Both Rachel and Terri anticipated a successful counseling process, and Terri had every confidence that her first treatment goals (as stated above) would be easily accomplished. It is not surprising, then, that at this stage in counseling, Terri's style as a therapist was a combination of S2 and S3. Much of the time Terri listened empathically to Rachel. But when specific bits of background information were needed or when Terri wanted to know more about Rachel's feelings than about her thoughts, an S2 stance was more appropriate. Terri was helping Rachel learn how to behave in therapy.

It is in this first stage of treatment that the therapist is answering assessment questions, deciding on what the client needs, and planning the course of treatment. This first step demonstrates the sequential nature of therapy. Other than in crisis situations, it is difficult to imagine when, in therapy, these two goals would not be among the early ones. The interactive nature of therapy will be seen later, as the therapist readjusts the treatment plan based on new information.

During the early therapy sessions, Terri learned quite a bit about Rachel's background and her current life. Rachel was the youngest of four children and the only daughter in a working-class family. Both parents had been employed at a local factory. Rachel's father had suffered from a degenerative disease which left him less and less able to provide for himself and his family. Her mother, by temperament and by circumstance, had been the primary strength in the family. In some ways Rachel was considered "one of the boys," but in other ways she felt singled out and belittled by her father and brothers because she was a girl. Her school performance was average, and at the end of high school Rachel drifted into a marriage with her high school sweetheart because "I couldn't think of anything else to do and I was fed up with living at home." Her new husband was a carpenter. She got a job in a local bank and worked there in a clerical position until her divorce seven years later.

Rachel blames her in-law situation for the breakup of her marriage. Her husband's parents were demanding, and her husband was unable to fight them. In time, Rachel got fed up with her in-laws' demands and her husband's passivity. She was particularly angry because her husband would be quite domineering with her while unable to assert himself with his parents. She began dreaming of both a divorce and a college education. By the time she announced that she was leaving the marriage, she had no question about the correctness of her decision. She said that she had never once looked back or had any regrets about the divorce.

After the divorce, Rachel kept her job and finished college. Her degree took six years to complete, and she managed to work and finish school by taking classes in all her spare time. It was at this point in her life that Rachel flowered intellectually. She loved college, loved learning, loved the social life that revolved around the university, and loved her new competence. She became an excellent student. Armed with her bachelor's degree, Rachel was able to leave her clerical job and get a part-time position at the university while completing her master's degree. Her friends were now mostly young graduate students and some professional people instead of the blue-collar friends of old. Women friends were plentiful and she dated a lot. However, for a number of years she did not wish to settle down again with anyone.

During this period, her father died of his degenerative illness and her mother was unexpectedly killed in an accident at the factory where she worked. Rachel had been close to her mother but, while saddened by this loss, had never really grieved.

Then, shortly after her mother's death, she met a man with whom she began to believe she could live forever. After fifteen months of serious dating, he announced he was leaving both the relationship and the community. Rachel kept a "stiff upper lip" about his announcement just as she had about her parents' death.

Rachel's current job appeared to be a plum but was, in fact, a lemon. Before taking this position, she had held a succession of short-term jobs, all of which had been varied and exciting. She thrived on challenges and diversity. By comparison, her current job was boring and limited. In addition to being bored, Rachel feared that she was dead-ended in this job and had nowhere to go. She was the only female in the organization and therefore suspected a sexist bias. Her distress with her employment situation had been growing over the past few months and was at a desperate point when she came in for help.

At the time she entered therapy, Rachel was involved in an affair with a married man. She and Ralph met while working together on a professional project. They had been lovers for a little over a year. For the most part, Rachel reported that the relationship had been working well for her. She had many interests, was involved in a variety of activities, and held a time-consuming job. Until recently, the undemanding nature of the relationship had been one of its virtues. Now, however, she had begun to realize that her biological clock was running down and was beginning to think about the possibility of children. Moreover, the secretive nature of the relationship was becoming more and more irritating to her. She was beginning to hate that they could never go out in public except under the guise of business. She was beginning to hate that they could never so much as touch hands in public. And she was beginning to hate the fact that they could never see each other on weekends.

Establishing the goals for therapy was a mutual decision involving a dialogue between Terri and Rachel. Terri used S3 therapist behavior for this goal-setting process. Both the therapist and the client recognized that the goals of therapy were going to be tied to career and relationship issues since depression was unusual for Rachel and seemed to be emanating from her work

situation and her unsatisfactory love affair. The therapeutic
career goal was obvious. Rachel needed to work on changing
jobs. The relationship task was much more complicated. What
exactly did Rachel want and need to accomplish? Did she want
to end this relationship or try to make it work? If not this man,
then who? And then what? The therapist pointed out that Rachel
had had a long history of disappointing relationships with men.
The initial relationship goal, then, became one of helping Rachel
to understand herself better—particularly understanding the
dynamics in her relationships with men. Once that goal was accomplished, Terri assumed that new tasks in this area might
be more readily determined (the interactional nature of therapy).

Given these goals, the therapist was now faced with questions about treatment planning. How could Terri assist Rachel
in completing these therapeutic tasks? As you know by now,
in the ACT model the answer to this question lies in determining the client's readiness level. Terri needed to evaluate Rachel's
willingness, ability, and confidence level for each of these goals
in order to provide the direction and structure necessary for goal
accomplishment.

Developing a Treatment Plan: Finding a New Job. Answers to
the questions for evaluating Rachel's willingness, ability, and
confidence for finding a new job all pointed to a high readiness
level for this therapeutic task. Rachel had previous experience
in applying for jobs, had previously prepared several résumés,
and had been interviewed for jobs on a number of occasions.
These past job-seeking efforts had been well rewarded. She had
never found it difficult to get a job. All of her role models were
employed and hardworking. Her current friends and associates
held responsible high-level positions. Rachel had many professional contacts within her field and in related fields. She had
no reluctance about using her network of friends and associates
in helping her find a new job. While Rachel was enthusiastic
about finding a different position, her current job involved
demanding work hours. Finding time for the job search was going to require some schedule juggling. Rachel's internal motivation was excellent. Her identity was inextricably bound to her

professional role, and finding a new job was a significant part of her focus at the time of therapy. As far as Terri could tell, the job-seeking task would in no way interfere with Rachel's coping mechanisms or defense systems. Only Rachel's confidence was less than optimal for the task at hand. The past year in her current position had eroded some of her basic work confidence a bit. Perhaps a good job search process and finding a new job would rejuvenate her confidence.

Rachel's readiness level related to support was not quite as high as her readiness level related to direction for the task of finding a new job. She was capable of providing some of her own support, but she also needed outside validation for this endeavor. Her friends and colleagues were highly supportive of a professional change, but her immediate work setting provided little support in the current job and would certainly provide none for the job-seeking process. Much of Rachel's support was expected to come from her numerous contacts in professional circles. She knew a lot of people and knew how to approach them for help and information. If the task itself went well, Rachel would garner support from the process.

All assessment indicators suggested a high readiness level to pursue a plan for changing jobs. The client knew how to go about finding a new job. She had the resources for the task. She wanted to find a new job. She had succeeded at this task in the past. At the moment her confidence about herself as a professional was a little lower than usual. Some outside support during the early phases of the process might be needed. An S4/S3 treatment approach was definitely indicated. Together, therapist and client established a goal of finding a new job (S3). Rachel developed her own plan for conducting the job search (S4). She would report to Terri about her progress from time to time (S4) and ask for support (S4/S3) if her spirit or her confidence was dragging. Terri made a mental note to provide unsolicited support (S3) early in Rachel's job-seeking process.

Developing a Treatment Plan: Relationships with Men. The issue of Rachel's relationships with men indicated a significantly different readiness profile. Rachel had little experience in trying to understand herself and little positive experience with men. She did, however, have very good relationships with women. Terri hoped that in time Rachel's ability to form intimate relationships with women would transfer to men. Rachel's friends and role models provided few good examples for healthy male/female relationships, however, and she had trouble citing any marriage she would like to emulate. Rachel's lover had little desire to see Rachel change in this regard. Rachel, too, had considerable ambivalence about working on this goal in therapy. Her unhappiness with the current state of affairs was balanced by her fear of being alone. She was not used to reflecting on her life, was not sure she would be successful at introspection and insight, and was even less certain that she wanted to invest much energy in a task that might not end in a permanent relationship. The therapist would surely need to provide significant direction.

Rachel also was going to need a lot of support to make progress on this therapeutic goal. It was unlikely that she would be capable of providing her own internal support for a task about which she was so ambivalent and so inexperienced. Terri did not expect Rachel's lover to support this enterprise, and support from friends was expected to be mixed. Rachel's self-sufficiency and involvement in a variety of activities would help carry her through a potentially difficult period. It was not anticipated that the task itself would be reinforcing at first.

The therapist's evaluation indicated that Rachel was not ready for the task of trying to understand herself and her relationships with men in such a way as to improve future functioning in this area. The contrast in readiness on the two therapeutic goals was noteworthy and signaled the need for the therapist to take two very different approaches. Rachel's R2 readiness level vis-à-vis the relationship issue suggested a structured treatment plan for this task. Terri planned to teach Rachel, through questions and observations, how to make connections between past and present events and how to examine the effect of situations and other people on herself. Some assignments would be given: information gathering through talking with family members and childhood friends; reconstructing events;

keeping a list of things she did or did not like about her lover; looking for new role models related to marriage; planning more social activities away from her lover; and so forth. The relationship between Terri and Rachel would be an important reinforcer in this process. Trust and liking would be essential. Rachel was going to need approval and support. The treatment plan for the second task was firmly rooted in an S2 approach.

The Therapy Process. Not surprisingly, therapy hours focused primarily on the task connected to relationships. The job change task required only that Rachel briefly report on progress in that area. As we looked back over case notes and reviewed some of the therapy tapes, it was possible to see how the therapy process evolved over the course of treatment.

In sessions 1 and 2, Terri gathered most of the background information on Rachel and began to form a therapeutic relationship conducive to progress. Initially Rachel was uncertain what was expected of her in therapy. She had little previous experience in self-examination. She was a quick student, however. Her brightness and high verbal ability were invaluable in her progress. By session 2, work on the therapeutic tasks was already beginning to proceed. Terri used a primarily S2/S3 stance in the early sessions. Her major goals at this point were to help Rachel relax about therapy, like and trust the therapist, and share confidences about herself. Rachel needed some direction about how to conduct herself in counseling and what kinds of information to share. A brief excerpt from session 2 typifies this stage of treatment:

Therapist:	So, what was it like to be the only daughter in your family?
Rachel:	Oh, you know, nothing special.
Therapist:	Wasn't it hard to be different? Like being the only kid in the family who wasn't on the high school football team?
Rachel:	Um, well, my dad was kind of macho— hunting and fishing—stuff like that. I used to wish he'd take me, but he only

took the boys. And I hated being the
one who had to wash dishes and help
with housework. My mom worked, so
I had an awful lot of household responsibilities.

Therapist: How do you think being the only daughter has affected you?

Rachel: I don't think it did.

Therapist: Take a few minutes and really think
about that.

Rachel: (Long pause.) Um, I was going to say
it didn't again. But, uh, I guess that's
not true. I think I resent men for keeping me from doing some things. And
I, uh, have a few unusual interests—
male kinds of interests. I work on my
own car you know, like a mechanic,
and I am into hang gliding as a hobby.
And, uh, even my job, I guess, is sort
of male-like.

Therapist: So in some ways being the only daughter got in your way and in others it
helped you? Expanded your horizons?

Rachel: Yeah!

Therapist: What about your ex-husband? Tell me
a little about the marriage.

Rachel: He was okay. But kind of macho! Except of course with his parents. He
thought as long as he brought home the
bacon, he was a good husband. I don't
even know what I wanted. But whatever it was, I didn't get it from him.
I spent more time with my friends than
with him.

Therapist: That must have been hard for you. It
sounds like you were married but still
alone. As I've listened to you, it sounds

	like you feel you can't depend on men. Your brothers left you out of things and then your husband didn't meet many of your needs. Now Ralph is only around on his terms and you can't depend on him for much. He can't or maybe won't even take you out to dinner.
Rachel:	(Pause.) I guess I never thought of it that way. I do sort of see a pattern.

In this client/therapist dialogue, you can see that Terri was directing therapy through the questioning process. At the same time, she was supportive of Rachel—reframing her family situation as having some good points as well as bad and understanding the loneliness of both her marriage and her relationship with her married lover, Ralph. The high level of support and the directiveness of the questions and interpretations were in the S2 mode. The interactive nature of therapy becomes very evident in this conversation. Terri began by getting background information. As Rachel's problem became easier to identify, Terri determined a goal for therapy and placed some of the emphasis of this early session on responding to the new goal. Now we turn to the opening of session 3 to see how treatment is developing:

Therapist:	So how was the week?
Rachel:	Fair. Every morning I feel kind of . . . almost sick as I head for work.
Therapist:	How are you progressing in looking for a job?
Rachel:	Pretty good. I did manage to get my résumé updated this week. I'm, uh, excited, but, uh, kind of nervous. I talked to a friend who is a vice president at one of the local companies and they are looking for someone for one of their east coast subsidiaries. They specifically

want a woman. My friend suggested
that I take the management testing they
offer to all prospective employees.

Therapist: That's great!

Rachel: He set it up for next Wednesday, so I'll
have to think of a way to take the morning off work. (Sighing.) This could
solve both my problems. If I got this
job, I'd have to move—so good-bye,
Ralphie.

Therapist: And the sigh?

Rachel: I'm not sure if I'd like to have Ralph
out of my life.

Therapist: Before we talk about you and Ralph,
tell me about the nervousness and ex-
citement related to the career testing.

Rachel: Well, the job stuff is a real high. But
I'm nervous that this testing will prove
I don't have what it takes to be a manager in a big corporation. I don't think
I'm typical. In some ways, uh, too
much like a woman—too focused on
people rather than on getting the job
done sometimes.

Therapist: It seems no matter how the testing turns
out, it will be helpful for you. After all,
if you wouldn't make a good manager
in a large corporation, then you probably wouldn't want the job anyway. It
would be too much like being where
you are now. Feeling devalued and
alone.

Rachel: Hum. I guess you're right. I, uh, hadn't
thought of it that way.

Therapist: (Waiting a moment or two.) Well, keep
me posted. How have things been with
Ralph since we last talked?

Terri's delegation of the job search activity is obvious in this excerpt. Terri provided a little support and almost no direction (S3). Rachel's high level of competence and motivation made delegation appropriate. At one point, Rachel began to turn her attention to the relationship with Ralph. But Terri briefly redirected her to the job search situation, sensing some yet unfinished business. Focusing on Rachel's feelings about the jobseeking process was important. Terri wanted to help Rachel be more attentive and expressive about her feelings. Once the job discussion was complete, Terri returned to working with Rachel on the issue of men.

The next several sessions continued in a similar manner with Rachel briefly reporting on the job situation. Most of the therapy time was spent on Rachel's relationships with the men in her life. In the sixth therapy hour, Rachel's increasing growth and development became clear to both therapist and client:

Rachel: I've been thinking for the past couple of weeks that I'm really not okay with the way things are with Ralph. (Long pause.) Sometimes when we're having lunch, I just want to touch him, you know. And I can't. Somebody might see us. Normal couples can touch each other. I asked him if we couldn't kind of get away for a couple of days together. I wanted to be able to talk this thing through. He said he'd see what he could arrange. He called back later and said that he thought he needed to get away alone. He said he really needs to decide whether or not to leave his wife. I think I'm sort of nervous about this relationship.

Therapist: Do you think some of your uncertainty is because if he leaves his wife, you might have to make a commitment?

Whenever we talk, I always hear a certain kind of, uh, comfort or a liking of the kind of relationship you have with Ralph. You can have some closeness and good sex but you are still free to live your own life. There's no one to report to.

Rachel: I think at some level I've known that about myself for some time. The trouble is I think I'm kind of changing. (Long pause.) There's more I haven't told you. I did what you suggested and went to that political rally on Tuesday night. Don't faint! I met a guy there and then had lunch with him yesterday. We're supposed to have dinner tomorrow night.

Therapist: (Laughing.) I might have suggested going to the rally, but I didn't know you were such a fast worker. Tell me about him.

Rachel: He's a different sort of guy than I usually fall for—a couple of years younger than me, and that bothered me at first, but lots of just plain fun. What's really different is that he is so nice to me. I'm real uncomfortable but I kind of like it. And we really hit it off talking together.

Therapist: What do you mean, nice?

Rachel: Oh, he tells me I'm attractive, that he likes my brains. I could almost gag telling you this, but he brought flowers to lunch yesterday. I've never gotten flowers before. It's so different from Ralph.

Therapist: Feeling disloyal?

Rachel: No. Why should I? Ralph and I have no agreement. It's just that I'm not

	used to this kind of attention. It embarrasses me, but it's kind of nice too.
Therapist:	What else about this man?
Rachel:	Well, he's got a so-so job. Trying to finish a degree at night and so in a lot of ways isn't into a career yet. I'm sure I make more money than he does. That's kind of different from most of the men I've met these past few years. Never been married. Comes from a problem family, though, I think. His sister was at the party. She seemed pretty weird. Drunk, I think! Jim thought so too. He told me his dad was an alcoholic. He died a few years back. Jim seems real kind and he's good company, um, a lot of fun, easy to really talk to. I like those things.
Therapist:	Well, I'll expect to hear more next week after your dinner date. Let me shift a little bit and ask you a different kind of question. Any ways that Jim and Ralph are alike? Or any qualities that you see in Jim, given you hardly know him yet, that remind you of your dad or your brothers?
Rachel:	(Long pause.) Well, um, Ralph and Jim both seem to like capable women. That'd be a laugh for my dad or my brothers. Or my ex for that matter. (Pause.) But Ralph and Jim seem so different to me. Although they both are good at talking. I don't know, do you think I'm overreacting to the things we've been talking about with Ralph and my dad and all? Like maybe rushing out and grabbing the first guy who seems different?

The Rachel of the sixth session was different from the Rachel of session 1. The most dramatic change was in her readiness (her willingness and her ability) to try to understand herself better. While basically a pragmatic, no-nonsense, don't have time to waste thinking about myself kind of person, Rachel was starting to think about herself in ways that Terri hoped would improve her life. This session illustrates Terri using mostly S3 therapist behavior, although occasionally she uses the art of questioning to redirect (S2) the focus. The remainder of the session was spent talking about dad, brothers, Ralph, and Jim—but mostly Rachel.

The following week Rachel announced that she had left the last session feeling bewildered and overwhelmed but that in the last few days, things had been becoming clearer. She knew she had to end the affair with Ralph—at least until Ralph made some decisions about his marriage.

Rachel: I told Ralph on Sunday night that I wasn't going to have sex with him for a while. We'll have to see each other because of work sometimes, and I said we could still have lunch on occasion, but I didn't want any kind of physical contact. I need to figure this out. He said he didn't like it but he did understand it. I'm beginning to think I deserve a better relationship. This thing with Jim must be getting to me.

Therapist: It must have been hard to tell Ralph that. Feeling proud of yourself?

Rachel: I think so. (Sighing.) Meeting Jim has confused some of this. I'm just surprised at how good it feels to have someone who is available and who really is trying to please me. Jim is, um, actually the first guy I've been with who really focuses on *me.* All in all, I'm feeling so much better than when I came

Therapist: in. I can't believe this could help like
this. Remember the week I suddenly
began crying because I missed my
mother? I felt ridiculous. She's been
dead years. But you were right, I felt
better after I cried—kind of, uh, silly,
but better.

Therapist: I'm glad things are perking up. By the
way, what's with the job?

Rachel: The thing with that company isn't going to work out. But I think I'm okay
with that. I've put out a lot of feelers
and several people have contacted me
because they heard I was looking for a
change. I guess I don't doubt that if I'm
patient, something good will turn up.
Funny, but that testing thing really
helped me. It gave me kind of a boost. I
think I was more anxious about it than I
admitted to myself. The feedback was
real helpful and real validating. I kind
of knew all those things about myself but
something . . . uh . . . something about
having someone important tell you all
that stuff is good. It was definitely
worth going through, even though the
job isn't going to pan out.

Rachel was more aware of herself and able to understand
her feelings and behavior. Best of all, she was regaining some
confidence and optimism. The depression was fading. In the
preceding dialogue, the style of therapy was shifting toward
delegation (S4). Rachel herself was taking more responsibility
for the direction of the hour and for providing her own support.

Rachel was not a woman to waste time. So it was no surprise to Terri when she proposed that they see each other every
few weeks instead of every week now that she was feeling so
much better. The therapist was not fooled into thinking all areas

of difficulty had been totally resolved at this point. Terri was certain, for example, that while selecting Jim was an improvement over previous choices in lovers, Rachel still needed growth in this area. But Terri deferred to Rachel's judgment about what she needed and therefore let Rachel make the decision regarding the frequency of therapy sessions (S4).

On the ninth visit, Rachel announced that she thought she was ready to terminate counseling. The decision was pure S4—totally delegated to the client. Terri let Rachel know that the door was open for any "booster shots" should they be necessary. Terri did not hear from Rachel again. She has, however, had a number of referrals from Rachel and through some of these referrals has inadvertently learned that Rachel appears to be getting along well. She has continued to climb the career ladder. Terri also hears occasional bits and pieces about Rachel's work through the media and mutual acquaintances. Terri has less information about Rachel's personal life. She does know, however, that Rachel has not married.

Rachel's relatively brief psychotherapy involved important ACT principles suggestive of successful counseling. Because Rachel's readiness level for her therapeutic goals varied, the treatment plan included a variety of therapist styles—sometimes S2, sometimes S3, and sometimes S4. The therapist tried to match her behavior to the client's readiness level and to move as the client moved. The treatment plan was neither arbitrary nor capricious. It was systematically selected to match the client's needs. And, apparently, the treatment worked—that is, it helped the client feel better because it helped her make changes that needed to be made.

Rachel, like a number of clients we see in voluntary outpatient psychotherapy, was self-referred. She sought counseling because she wanted to feel better. Not every client enters therapy in so self-directed a manner. A therapist's lot is a lot easier when he or she is counseling with willing and able clients. Often, if the therapist cannot motivate the unwilling client sufficiently there is no opportunity even to test his or her therapeutic finesse. If the client does not come for therapy, how can we be helpful? Our second goal for this chapter is to demonstrate the ways in which ACT can help the therapist who is dealing with a reluctant client.

The Client Who Didn't Want Counseling

Charlie's experience with his client Rich is a case in point. Rich was assigned to counseling after a drinking incident in a college residence hall. Apparently, Rich's obnoxious behavior under the influence of alcohol had been observed on several other occasions as well. Rich had been informed that if he wanted to continue to live in the dorm and stay in college, he had to see a counselor. This was a clear example of coercive power at work as, obviously, Rich was not very interested in being in therapy. But since it was important to Rich to stay in school, counseling appeared to be his only option. In the first session, he stated with no reluctance, "The only reason I'm here is because I have to be." Charlie correctly diagnosed the first therapeutic task as one of establishing some kind of relationship and credibility with the client. He needed a way to persuade Rich to become a willing participant in the process.

Charlie and his supervisor worked out a plan. Charlie assigned Rich the task of taking the MMPI (S1). Because Charlie was experienced and knowledgable with the MMPI, he was able to interpret the results to Rich in a way that let Rich know that Charlie understood him (S2). Through an on-target interpretation of the MMPI, Charlie was able to demonstrate his expertise. To Rich it almost seemed that Charlie was clairvoyant. The therapist had immediate credibility.

This was expert power at work! The power bases early in Rich's therapy were expert power, coercive power, and position power. Rich, an unwilling client, needed a "stick" in order even to come for therapy. He needed to have faith in the curative agent in order to continue attending. And he needed to believe that this therapist was in a position to put in a good word for him with residence hall personnel.

At this point in the therapy process, the therapist and the client had different goals for therapy. The therapist was trying to build trust, establish a relationship, and get Rich involved in the change process. Rich, on the other hand, wanted to please the therapist so he could get out of therapy and stay in the dorm. Rich approached his goal by telling the therapist exactly what he thought the therapist wanted to hear. On the surface, this was the quickest cure imaginable. Like most quick cures, this one did not last long and, predictably, Rich did not bother to show up for the fourth and fifth sessions. Charlie had erroneously moved too quickly to using S2/S3 behavior in the third session. Rich, for all intents and purposes, was still unwilling to participate in therapy. Charlie misinterpreted Rich's words as true expressions of his feelings and motivation. Rich needed more direction and less support because his readiness level for therapy was still quite low. Style 1 was still the treatment style of choice.

After two no-shows, Charlie, in conference with his supervisor, determined that more structure would be required if Rich were to continue therapy long enough to become truly involved in the counseling process and in changing his problematic behavior. Consequently, Charlie wrote a formal letter to Rich stating, in no uncertain terms, that if Rich did not recontact Charlie immediately to set up an appointment, Charlie would report Rich to the appropriate university personnel for breach of contract. Rich, of course, responded by immediately making another appointment with Charlie. When he arrived for the session, Rich was quietly furious. Charlie gave him permission to be angry, and out of this first honest interaction the therapist and the client finally agreed upon a therapy contract. Wisely, Charlie had moved from the S1 stance of the letter to the S2 stance of supporting Rich's anger and negotiating a mutually acceptable therapy contract. Charlie reframed Rich's problem in such a way that it was acceptable to Rich. According to Charlie, Rich had not learned the appropriate behavior for group living. The goal of counseling, therefore, was going to be to help him learn new behavior that would allow him to live in the residence hall without incident. This social learning contract was a clear S2 treatment plan.

In the course of expressing his anger at Charlie's letter, Rich inadvertently revealed a repressed rage aimed at his family. Charlie's personal hypothesis, which began to develop in this session, was that Rich was unable to deal directly with his anger at his parents and might be using alcohol as a coping mechanism to relieve some of the pressure of the unexpressed anger. It also occurred to Charlie that Rich's drinking might be a passive-aggressive way to strike back at his parents.

By applying ACT principles to this case, Charlie concluded that it would be unwise to share this hypothesis with Rich
at this time. Charlie had learned that it was a mistake to let
up on direction too early with Rich. An S3 approach to therapy
might be useful later, but counseling needed to focus now on
assisting Rich to control unacceptable behavior that was likely
to get him into trouble. The mutually agreed upon social learning contract would, if successfully carried out, meet the goals
of the university, the client, and the therapist. Rich participated
in a social skills group (S2) in addition to attending individual
counseling sessions with Charlie. In time, he successfully changed
some of his behavior.

Rich's relationship with Charlie continued to improve.
Ever so slowly, the power bases for the therapist shifted from
coercive, expert, and position power to personal and reward
power. Rich found himself liking Charlie and wanting his approval. The developmental nature of the treatment process is
readily observed when one thinks about Rich's stance early in
therapy and then looks at an excerpt from a therapy session conducted about five months later. Charlie and Rich had been talking about Rich's family:

Rich:	For a brief period of time, yes, there was a normal family there, but a lot of those memories have been overshadowed by all the other lousy things that happened. There was a lot of craziness in my family.
Charlie:	You didn't really . . . didn't have much preparation in your upbringing for fitting into society, did you?
Rich:	Yep. (Pause.) That hits it right on the head.
Charlie:	That alone could stir up a lot of anger and resentment in you. It's sort of like . . . like a legacy that you carry with you even today.
Rich:	(Long pause.) Uh-huh.
Charlie:	I was thinking about this after we talked last time. When I think about your back-

ground and everything you've told me about your family, the thing that really impresses me is that you're one hell of a survivor. Did you ever stop to think that now that you're in college, in spite of your past, you've really kind of pulled yourself up?

Rich: That thought has kind of struck me a couple of times.

Charlie: Feels pretty good, doesn't it?

Rich: (Pause.) Well, it's like I said. I enjoyed myself before, but when I compare working at that shitty job with being here in school, I think I have a much better chance at moving upward—earning a lot more money, you know.

Charlie: The really interesting thing to me, you know, with your background is how easy it would have been to drift off to another kind of life.

Rich: Like my brother did?

Charlie: Yeah! You haven't done that. I'm sure there must have been a tremendous pull to do that. Just to surrender and give up and say, "Hell, I can't have anything good in life so I might as well just accept things the way they are."

Rich: I think I'm really kind of disgusted by people like my brother . . . the scumbags of the world.

Charlie: You're making a good effort to become something. Academically, you're right on target. Socially, it feels like you are finally making some strides. It was healthy for you to break away from your family and get out on your own and try to make it. Do you have any thoughts about that?

Rich: (Long pause.) One of the first thoughts

	is that you're one of the first people to have looked at it that way.
Charlie:	Really! How do others picture it?
Rich:	I guess not many other people have as much knowledge about me as you do. There's times I feel like I'm slowly overcoming all the things I learned. And times that the vastness of all the things I have to overcome still . . .
Charlie:	There's a lot of work to be done, isn't there? But the fact that you've accomplished so much convinces me that there's a lot more you can do.

Imagine this S3 conversation taking place when just a number of months earlier Charlie needed threatening letters just to get Rich to show up for counseling! Yet most practitioners have witnessed similar transformations in their own practices. Sometimes therapy is like a dance between therapist and client that takes them through a series of steps to the other side of the ballroom. With Rich and Charlie, the steps progressed one at a time from an S1 position (where Charlie provided most of the direction and the therapeutic contingencies provided most of the support) to an S4 position many months later. Eventually Rich was able to direct and support himself both in therapy and in life. But if Charlie had not mobilized his abilities to be a highly directive (S1) therapist, none of Rich's growth would have been possible.

The ACT model holds that each therapeutic task, as well as the entire therapeutic process, can be viewed as this same kind of dance. The variety of tasks or goals in therapy is endless. Some of these tasks relate to helping a well-functioning client progress to an even higher level of functioning. Some tasks focus on assisting the client to maintain a current level of functioning— not to fall backward. And some therapeutic tasks relate to the tiny incremental steps that help a seriously impaired person to move ahead. ACT can be useful in a variety of different therapeutic contexts.

The Client Who Said Good-bye to Hallucinations

Our final two goals in demonstrating the application of ACT to clinical cases are to illustrate the utility of ACT in working with a psychotic individual, a person taking tiny therapeutic steps, and to demonstrate how ACT can be used in structuring treatment around one specific therapeutic task. One of the authors has been working with a significantly disturbed lady for several years. The therapy is composed of numerous different tasks, and the client, whom we will call Sheila, is at different readiness levels for the various tasks. One of the most important therapy goals is for Sheila to stay in touch with reality—not always an easy task for a woman who is prone to imagining voices and hallucinating. For the past three years, Sheila has successfully held a part-time job and she is determined not to let her problems interfere with the responsible execution of her duties. This is the first decent job that Sheila has had, and it has helped her self-esteem enormously.

Sheila and the therapist have agreed that one of the ongoing goals in therapy is for Sheila to be able to control her "freaking out," her losing touch with reality, her hallucinations. In describing the treatment plan and the progress pertaining to Sheila's goal to control her hallucinations, we illustrate the application of ACT in treating specific psychotic problems.

The therapeutic goal, in this case, was to be able to control hallucinations. Sheila, who had a long psychiatric history including six years in a state mental hospital, wanted desperately to conquer this problem because her job had become very important to her. In other words, there was little overt problem related to willingness although the therapist suspected that the hallucinations served some important psychological purpose and there might be unconscious resistance to giving them up. Sheila's ability to stop hallucinating was an entirely different matter. In the early phases of working on this task, Sheila would often say, "If I knew how to stop them, I would have stopped them long ago. They just take over and I can't make them go away."

All the assessment data pertaining to this task indicated that treatment would have to begin at the S1 level. A plan was mapped out and shared with Sheila. The following excerpt from therapy illustrates the therapist's structuring of the treatment:

Therapist: Sheila, do you have enough control when you start hearing voices to talk rationally to yourself?

Sheila: I don't know.

Therapist: Let's try something new! When you hear voices, I want you to say, "My mother is dead. She is not here in this room." I want you to say that over and over again until the voice stops. Do you think you can do that?

Sheila: I can try. But I don't know if it will work.

Therapist: Do you ever hear your mother's voice when you are here with me?

Sheila: Sometimes.

Therapist: I want you to tell me the next time that happens so that you can practice talking to yourself here. Okay?

Sheila: Okay.

By the next session, the therapist concluded that Sheila was not able to talk to herself in such a way as to stop the voices. Sheila was then instructed to call the therapist whenever the voices started while she was at work (S1). If unavailable, the therapist promised to return the call as soon as possible. The therapist only needed to give Sheila a minute or two of structured directions by phone. Sheila would call and say, "Tell me something helpful." That was a signal to the therapist that Sheila was struggling with the voices. The therapist firmly would say, "Your mother is not there. Your mother is dead. She cannot possibly be there. She cannot possibly hurt you. Look around the room. Your mother is not there, right?" And after a moment or two, Sheila would agree, thank the therapist, and hang up.

At this point in the therapy, there was no focus on seeking to understand the meaning of the voices or interpreting their meaning to Sheila (S3). Sheila certainly was not yet ready for insight therapy. What she needed was help in controlling behavior that could cost her a job and perhaps send her back to the state hospital. The therapist maintained a strong S1 stance throughout this stage of treatment, providing a great deal of direction related to the task. The therapist's directions involved telling Sheila exactly what to say to herself, telling her that her mother was not there, telling her to remember that she was sitting at work and if she was sitting at work it must be 1985 and her mother must be dead, telling her to feel her wristwatch (which she bought *after* her mother had died), and telling her to put on her earphones and listen to classical music, which usually drowned out the voices. The key word here is *telling*. The therapist had assessed that Sheila could not manage much of her own therapy at this point.

Before long, however, Sheila and the therapist began to engage in a bit more dialogue (S2) about the process of rational self-talk related to the imaginary voice of Sheila's mother. Now, when Sheila would call because she was struggling with the voices, the conversation would be slightly different. It usually would go something like this:

Sheila: Tell me something helpful.

Therapist: Sheila, what do you think I would tell you?

Sheila: That my mother isn't here.

Therapist: Right. It's good you know what I'd say. Can you say that to yourself?

Sheila: My mother isn't here?

Therapist: Try saying it like it isn't a question.

Sheila: My mother isn't here.

Therapist: Good. What else?

Sheila: (Pause.) I'm here at work so she can't be alive?

Therapist: Very good. I'm very proud of you. You have really learned to start to talk to yourself in a good way. Try to do that for yourself. But if you need a little reminder, feel free to give me a call.

The therapist had moved (and that movement had been gradual, one step at a time) to the S2 position in terms of this therapeutic goal. A significant support component had been added, and the therapist was teaching Sheila how to take over rational self-talk for herself. Sheila was learning how to ground herself in reality—how not to "freak out."

As therapy progressed, the therapist's style on this task continued to move one step at a time to the S3 position. Sheila and the therapist talked about how Sheila was doing. There was still some direction from the therapist, but it was diminishing in specificity. "You can tell yourself those things now, right, Sheila?" And there was a great deal of support and positive reinforcement for Sheila's progress. The therapist remembered to tell Sheila things like, "I am proud of you." "That was great." "You did a good job of fighting off the voices this week." When Sheila slipped, as she sometimes did, the therapist moved back one step at a time to provide the structure and the support that was missing.

As Sheila moved toward self-sufficiency in terms of controlling the voices and staying grounded in reality, the therapist was continuing to withdraw both direction and support. For a while, Sheila reported that she was handling the voices herself now and the therapist provided whatever reinforcement Sheila seemed to be needing. In time, the reports got fewer and farther between. Eventually, so gradually it was almost imperceptible, the therapist realized that none of the therapy time was being spent dealing with hallucinations. Sheila's goal on this task had been met. The course of the treatment in meeting that goal can be seen in Figure 8.

At this point in the treatment process, the therapist is prepared for the fact that new and different therapy goals related to the hallucinating might emerge later. Therapy might eventually focus on Sheila's relationship with her mother, for example. One of the factors determining the future foci of treatment would be whether to work with Sheila adaptively or structurally (Gordon and Beresin, 1983). In Debra's case, described in Chapter Six, the decision was made for intensive restructuring. Sheila's age, history, and so forth would need to be taken into account in this treatment decision.

Figure 8. ACT Treatment for Controlling Hallucinations.

Therapist supports client for using rational self-talk Example: "Great! You did a good job of talking to yourself." Q3	**Therapist teaches client how to talk to herself more rationally** Example: "What would I tell you? Very good." Q2
Q4 **Client takes care of herself and reports progress to therapist** Example: "I was able to stop the voices yesterday."	Q1 **Therapist tells client what to say to herself and what to do** Example: "Tell yourself that your mother is dead."

The purpose of this chapter was to demonstrate how to translate ACT principles into therapeutic practice. ACT is designed to help the eclectic clinician select the best possible treatment plan for the client. The best possible treatment plan, of course, is the plan with the greatest likelihood for success. All the cases presented in this chapter utilized ACT in the treatment planning process. In the next chapter we present some therapy cases in which treatment was not knowingly planned using the ACT framework. We will describe a number of cases reported in the literature by well-seasoned therapists in order to back up our contention that good therapy uses ACT principles even when the therapist is not aware of the model.

9

♯ ♯ ♯ ♯ ♯ ♯ ♯ ♯ ♯ ♯ ♯ ♯ ♯

How ACT
Sheds New Light
on Old Cases

One of the reviewers from an earlier article about ACT raised what we thought was an interesting question. He asked if ACT could be used to explain successful therapy cases already reported in the literature. After all, he went on to say, the authors use ACT principles in their own practices and in their own supervision and training, so one would expect their examples of therapy to follow ACT principles. But they are contending that good therapists *intuitively* use their model. They believe that part of the value of this model is in giving conceptual understanding to those things that good therapists do almost instinctively. If good therapists naturally adhere to ACT, the literature ought to be able to confirm this.

His point was well taken. In formulating our model, we had already engaged in an informal research project to see if indeed the case literature would indicate that successful therapy uses ACT principles. In the course of our normal reading, we had been reading case histories with an eye to seeing if the ACT model fit. While our reading would not qualify as a statistically sound research design, our cases could, in some ways, be considered to be randomly selected. Whatever case we had in hand became a case to which we tried to apply ACT. Occasionally, we sought out cases from specific theoretical perspectives to see if our contentions were accurate from a variety of orientations to psychotherapy. What we discovered did not surprise us. In general, cases in the literature that reported successful therapeutic outcomes adhered to ACT principles and could easily be explained in ACT terms.

In this chapter we present some of these cases from the literature and discuss the relationship between these cases and our ACT model. Since all the cases in the following section were described before publication of our first ACT article, we feel safe in stating that none of the authors was familiar with the ACT model at the time of the therapy or the writing. We have tried to cite cases from the literature that represent a variety of theoretical positions and therapeutic purposes. We believe that ACT has a broad-based potential for structuring therapy and that the application of ACT can assist therapists from differing theoretical backgrounds and therapists working in a variety of treatment settings, as well as being a tool for the eclectic practitioner. Apart from illustrating how easily the ACT model can explain the successful practice of psychotherapy, this chapter also demonstrates that no matter what theoretical framework a therapist employs, good therapy insists that the clinician provide treatment that fits the client's readiness level.

Case Example: Cognitive-Behavioral Therapy

As you may recall from Chapter Three, many of the behavioral approaches to psychotherapy can best be described as falling within the S1 and S2 modes of treatment. One of the areas in which behavioral techniques have been successful is in working with populations of seriously disturbed individuals. This success would be predictable according to the ACT model. It is not unreasonable to assume that the more disturbed a person is, the less ready he or she will be in terms of general readiness for therapy. Several cases from the literature illustrate the value of the S1 and S2 therapist styles for working with the seriously impaired. The first of these cases involves a cognitive-behavioral treatment approach.

Meichenbaum (1977) discusses the value of self-instructional training in order to deal with such difficulties as the impulsivity of hyperactive and aggressive children or the cognitive functioning of schizophrenics. An impulsive hyperactive child is generally at an R1 or R2 level of readiness for tasks that require extended concentration. Such a child may be unwilling and unable or may be willing but unable to perform such tasks. The process of teaching an impulsive child to modify his or her behavior would be in an S2 mode according to ACT. The child needs to be *taught* a different way to behave. Meichenbaum and Goodman (1971) suggest that the new learning will be accomplished by an adult talking to himself while performing the task to be learned by the child, the child performing the task with specific guidance from the adult, and the child then performing the task while talking to himself. The treatment plan is a perfect metaphor for the ACT model. At the beginning of treatment, direction and support are provided by the adult teacher. By the end of the process, if treatment has been successful, the child will be self-instructing in terms of the task to be performed. Direction and support will be internalized—delegated (S4).

In the excerpt that follows, the adult is performing the task while talking to himself aloud in order to model self-instruction for the child. Notice how the adult model gives specific directions and high levels of support (S2) in the first phase of a process of trying to teach the willing but unable hyperactive child how to copy a lined pattern:

Okay, what is it I have to do? You want me to copy the picture with the different lines. I have to go slowly and carefully. Okay, draw the line down, down, good; then to the right, that's it; now down some more and to the left. Good, I'm doing fine so far. Remember, go slowly. Now back up again. No, I was supposed to go down. That's okay. Just erase the line carefully. . . . Good. Even if I make an error I can go on slowly and carefully. I have to go down now. Finished. I did it! [Meichenbaum, 1977, p. 32]

The high-direction/high-support self-instruction that the adult is providing as a teaching model for the child is very much in keeping with what ACT would recommend for a treatment process in which the client is mostly willing but unable. Structure and support are both necessary in the performance of a task. In the early phase of the process, the adult teacher is responsible for providing the direction and support. Teaching self-instruction should eventually permit the child not only to remind himself how to complete the specific task of copying a line pattern but also to provide his own support. The intention of the treatment plan is that at some point the child will have been delegated the responsibility for performing the task. When he can complete the task by instructing himself, he will in essence have progressed from a low level of task readiness to a high level.

Case Example: Reality Therapy

Glasser (1965, p. 111), reporting on hospital treatment for psychotic patients, describes a reality therapy program instituted by Dr. G. L. Harrington in the Veterans Administration Neuropsychiatric Hospital in Los Angeles as follows:

> Dr. Harrington instituted the Reality Therapy program when he took over Building 206. Rather than concentrating on making the patient happy, the program stressed carefully graded increments of responsibility so that the patient could slowly work his way back to reality. The building was divided into a fifty-man closed ward, a fifty-man semi-open ward, and a one-hundred-man open ward. All personnel, including clerk-typist, clothing-room clerk, aides, nurses, social worker, and psychologist, were given responsibilities of reporting behavior concerning the patients' readiness for movement either in the direction of greater or lesser responsibility. During a regular building meeting attended by both staff and patients, patient prob-

lems were discussed, ward assignments were made (usually along the progression from closed to semi-open to open ward states), and the individual patient programs were established.

We are struck by the one-step-at-a-time progressive nature of the program and even by the use of the term *readiness* in Glasser's description of this program. The treatment plan clearly matches the guidelines for treatment planning spelled out by ACT. And the entire treatment program is well suited to the readiness level of the population for which it is geared.

We also found it interesting to read Glasser's (1965) description of several incidents that indicate the importance of providing sufficient external direction and structure for the less ready patient. In one way or another, such a patient will often insist that the treatment provide the direction he needs. Glasser describes a patient from the closed ward who asked for a pass to go into town. When his request was denied, the patient thanked the doctor. Another patient, who had not been assigned to the closed ward, asked for a transfer to the maximum security unit of the VA hospital. He happily settled for a reclassification to closed-unit status.

Case Example: Crisis Counseling

An individual case reported by Getz, Wiesen, Sue, and Ayers (1974, p. 136) describes a twenty-three-year-old woman who had been treated in an emergency room in the throes of a panic attack. When she appeared for counseling the following day, she was calm, cooperative, and did not appear at all upset. In the meeting with the counselor, the client gave some suggestion of psychotic behavior. Here is an excerpt from what might be termed the assessment interview:

Counselor: What finally made you go to the hospital last night?
Client: My thoughts weren't straight. They

were confused. I kept getting a pro-
phecy, and I kept writing down everything that came to my mind. My aunt
says that that's not right. So she called
a pastor. So I talked to him, and then
when I got real bad he came over and
tried to talk to me about it some more.
Then I felt at peace about it and went
to sleep, but then the next morning I
was back the same way again. . . . Just
like the devil was on the outside of me
this time—you know—and he was trying to get in there and taunt me of those
pasts that I have had.

Counselor: Could you see him?
Client: Well, not clearly.
Counselor: Could you hear him?
Client: The voice was the thoughts.
Counselor: Were the voices coming from inside or from outside?
Client: From inside.
Counselor: What were they saying?

While it is clear that the client is willing to talk with the counselor, her psychotic state makes her ability suspect. The counselor does an excellent job of moving to very specific questions
in order to provide the client with some structure for telling about
her experience.

In discussing the treatment plan for this case, the authors
describe treatment that included Mellaril and the client's being assigned to the day-care program of the mental health center.
The day-care program was a closely supervised alternative to
hospitalization. Both the drug treatment and the partial hospitalization fall into the category of highly directive treatments.
This case, as would be anticipated by ACT, provided the appropriate structure and direction to match the assessed level of
client readiness.

Case Example: Client-Centered Therapy

The father of client-centered therapy, Carl Rogers, was already organizing his ideas about counseling in his early writings. At a used-book sale not long ago, one of the authors picked up Rogers's book *Counseling and Psychotherapy* (1942). Almost forty-five years ago, the young Rogers wrote (p. 115): "Before proceeding to further discussion of the process of therapy, it may be well to consider a basic objection which many will raise to the preceding chapters and which will apply equally to the chapters that follow. This objection is essentially that in counseling and psychotherapy as it has been described, and in the counseling relationship as pictured in the last chapter, the counselor takes no responsibility for directing the outcome of the process."

The seeds of client-centered therapy were already firmly planted and only needed nurturing to come to fruition. ACT contends that client-centered therapy has a place in treatment, but it is most helpful to the client who is at a readiness level that will enable him to profit from it. ACT classifies client-centered therapy as a therapy using mostly S3 therapist behavior. We turn now to the opening of the first interview with the client, Herbert Bryan, as it appears in Rogers's book (1942, pp. 265–268). We have eliminated Rogers's numbering system for easier reading in this quotation:

> *Counselor:* Well, now we were so concerned yesterday about these various aspects of whether or not we were to go ahead with it that I don't know that I have as clear a picture as I'd like to have of what's on your mind, so go ahead and tell me.
>
> *Subject:* Well, as accurately as I can convey the idea, I would term it a blocking which had manifestations in several fields.
>
> *Counselor:* M-hm.
>
> *Subject:* The—in my earlier childhood the symp-

tom of blocking which was emphasized
on my consciousness most was in
speech. I developed a speech impediment along about the sixth grade.
Then, as I matured, I noticed a blocking in sexual relations. However, not
in the voyeuristic situation, only in an
intercourse situation; oftentimes I had
difficulty there. Also an unpleasant
tight feeling in the lower abdomen, as
if, to use an analogy, there were some
sort of a cold, hard axe or some other
such thing pressing against the libido
in such a way as to block it.

Counselor: M-hm.

Rather than continuing to quote the entire dialogue between the counselor and the subject, we will repeat only the next
ten counselor responses (Rogers, 1942, pp. 265–268) because
they give such an excellent flavor of therapist style in an S3
position:

Counselor: M-hm. And does it cause you more
distress than it used to, or is that no
different?

Counselor: M-hm.

Counselor: M-hm. M-hm.

Counselor: A feeling of real pain, is that what you
mean?

Counselor: M-hm.

Counselor: And you say that you feel this does
block you in a good many areas of life?

Counselor: M-hm.

Counselor: M-hm. So that both in your work and
in your recreation you feel blocked.

Counselor: You just feel rather unable to do things,
is that it?

> *Counselor:*   M-hm. And you—in spite of the dif-
> ficulty that it causes you, you feel pretty
> sure that it isn't physical?

The counselor who is working with Bryan uses many "m-hms," which indicate that he is listening and following the subject. Moreover, responses by the counselor tend to clarify what the subject is saying. ACT claims that attentive, reflective listening is most valuable when it is used with the ready client. Now let us see what Rogers (pp. 263–264) has to say about Herbert Bryan: "He stated that he wished help with his problems and that he regarded them as deep-seated. . . . However, it might be added that Mr. Bryan turned out to be a highly intelligent, definitely neurotic young man, verbalistic and intellectual in his interests. This last trait makes his interviews particularly valuable, in that he verbalizes attitudes which most clients probably hold, but which few of them state with such clarity."

We are in agreement with Rogers that client-centered therapy is the most appropriate therapy style for this case because of the client's characteristics. We firmly believe that the same counselor style applied to a less ready client would be totally inappropriate. This case reported by Rogers had a successful outcome. We believe the success is attributable not only to good counselor skills but to the fact that the counselor's S3 style matched the needs of the client. Again, this is consistent with ACT.

Case Examples: Psychoanalysis

We have described psychoanalysis as a low-directive/low-supportive style of therapy in an earlier chapter. Its nondirectiveness is the result of psychodynamic therapy focusing on the client's agenda. Its nonsupportiveness comes from the strong belief of its proponents that the therapist must maintain strict objectivity regarding the client. In his book on dynamic psychiatry, Wallace (1983) shares a number of case vignettes in the course of describing theory and treatment. The following interaction (1983, p. 287) took place with a client who had recently moved some distance from the therapist. He had been in treatment ten months prior to moving. The client had spent the first half hour of the session behaving angrily.

> *Therapist:* What are you mad at me about?
>
> *Patient:* I'm mad at you because, because, because—well, simply because I come here. When your office was a five-minute walk away it was easier to believe these sessions aren't all that important. I could even pretend coming here was mechanical, out of habit, rather than from free choice. But now, now that I have to drive an hour and a half, three days a week, for these sessions at this ungodly early hour, I can't believe that any more. You see, every time I drive down here it reaffirms your importance to me.
>
> *Therapist:* And what's troublesome about that?
>
> *Patient:* (Silence) Well, partly because now you know about it too (silence—shifts nervously).
>
> *Therapist:* Yes, and what is it about that?
>
> *Patient:* Because I'm vulnerable, because I'm putting all my eggs in one basket, getting close to you to the exclusion of others, that makes me feel vulnerable. It's not safe. It's not good for me (silence).
>
> *Therapist:* Will you talk more about the danger?
>
> *Patient:* Well, it's not safe to get too close to one person. Then you're kind of at their mercy. I mean, you can be affected by what they do. Like if they leave or don't like you (silence).
>
> *Therapist:* So, you're telling me that if you draw close to me I might leave or not like you.

The low-support aspect of the session is clear in that the therapist does little to relieve or normalize the client's fears. He in no way comforts the client. The directive dimension of this brief dialogue is more confusing to dissect, however. Wallace describes the therapist's behavior as asking questions to discern meaning. There is a certain directiveness in such therapist behavior. In some ways, it is more leading than Rogers's "m-hm's," for example. On the other hand, the questions themselves do very little to direct the client. They are simply the restatement in question form of the client's previous remarks.

This client can be assessed as having a high readiness level for the general task of psychodynamic therapy. In this brief instance, the therapeutic task is to discern what his anger is all about. Even if we did not know that this client had been in intensive psychotherapy for at least ten months, his ability to talk about his anger is indicative of a high readiness level in understanding and sharing his feelings. The S4 behavior of the therapist is appropriate to the R4 level of the client.

A second case illustrates the importance of the relationship of the psychoanalytic process to the client's readiness level. Thomas Szasz (1959, p. 81) describes the client he selects to exemplify his former psychoanalytic approach to therapy in this way: "'K' was a man of mature years engaged in a complicated profession for which he had undergone prolonged training and preparation. His intelligence was superior, his appearance was pleasant, and his interest in helping himself through analysis, once he embarked upon it, was both earnest and persistent." From Szasz's description, we have every reason to believe that "K" is an appropriate candidate for an S4 treatment approach. What is especially interesting about this case is that "K" was an exhibitionist who upon being arrested for indecent exposure was given the coercive ultimatum that charges would only be dropped if he sought treatment. The likelihood of finding a willing and able client under these circumstances would seem to be remote. What made "K" an appropriate candidate for S4 treatment were the following facts: he had wanted help for quite some time but was fearful of seeking it; his arrest appeared to be self-determined, perhaps as a way to get help for himself;

he seized on the idea of treatment with no resistance; and he possessed the personal characteristics that made him an acceptable candidate for psychoanalysis.

Case Example: Systematic Desensitization

Systematic desensitization is theoretically a long way from psychoanalysis on the directive continuum. The client for whom systematic desensitization is the treatment of choice is frequently the phobic client who, at least in terms of the phobia, feels unable to control his or her own behavior and therefore seeks outside assistance. Because the phobic behavior feels so powerful, the client needs the therapist to take control and direct the therapy process. Systematic desensitization is a very specific, step-by-step sort of treatment.

Lazarus (1971) emphasizes that therapist flexibility and versatility are very important since individual patients should be matched with best-fitting therapists and therapies. This is certainly in keeping with our contentions. The phobic client is much more than just his or her phobic behavior. ACT would predict that successful therapists from specific behavioral orientations use varying styles depending on the task they are working on with the client and depending on the client's readiness level. Lazarus seems to agree, as can be seen in one of his case illustrations. The case provides an excellent example of the importance of matching therapist style with client readiness, and the match fits according to ACT principles. The client wanted to try systematic desensitization in order to get over a phobic fear of bridges. The therapist in this case does an excellent job of combining S2 and S3 behavior in order to gain an understanding of the client's problem. At this point, then, the therapist's task is to understand the client's phobic behavior. The client is willing and able to share information with the therapist. We pick up the therapist/client dialogue at the point where the client has already described having a fear of crossing bridges and has just asked the therapist if he ever consulted in the city, because in order to get to the therapist's office the client has to cross the Golden Gate bridge:

Therapist:	No. But tell me, how long have you had this problem?
Patient:	Oh, about four years, I'd say. It just happened suddenly. I was coming home from work and the Bay Bridge was awfully slow. I just suddenly panicked for no reason at all. I mean, nothing like this had ever happened to me before. I felt that I would crash into the other cars. Once I even had a feeling that the bridge would cave in.
Therapist:	Let's get back to that first panic experience about four years ago. You said that you were coming home from work. Had anything happened at work?
Patient:	Nothing unusual.
Therapist:	Were you happy at work?
Patient:	Sure! Huh! I was even due for promotion.
Therapist:	What would that have entailed?
Patient:	An extra $3,000 a year.
Therapist:	I mean in the way of having to do different work.
Patient:	Well, I would have been a supervisor. I would have had more than fifty men working under me.
Therapist:	How did you feel about that?
Patient:	What do you mean?
Therapist:	I mean how did you feel about the added responsibility? Did you feel that you were up to it, that you could cope with it?
Patient:	Gee! My wife was expecting our first kid. We both welcomed the extra money.
Therapist:	So round about the time that you were about to become a father, you were to be promoted to supervisor. So you would face two new and challenging

roles. You'd be a daddy at home and also big daddy at work. And this was when you began to panic on the bridge, and I guess you never did wind up as supervisor.

Patient: No. I had to ask for a transfer to the city.

Therapist: Now, please think very carefully about this question. Have you ever been involved in any accident on or near a bridge, or have you ever witnessed any serious accident on or near a bridge?

Patient: Not that I can think of.

Therapist: Do you still work for the same company?

Patient: No. I got a better offer, more money from another company in the city. I've been with them for almost one and a half years now.

Therapist: Are you earning more or less money than you would have gotten in Berkeley?

Patient: About the same. But prices have gone up so it adds up to less.

Therapist: If you hadn't developed the bridge phobia and had become foreman in Berkeley at $3,000 more, where do you think you would be today?

Patient: Still in Berkeley.

Therapist: Still supervisor? More money?

Patient: Oh hell! Who knows? (laughs) Maybe I would have been vice-president? [Lazarus, 1971, pp. 33–35]

This conversation between therapist and client involves mostly S2 and a few S3 behaviors on the part of the therapist. The therapist structures many of the questions in order to gather the needed information (S2). At the same time, we see several therapist remarks aimed at clarifying and interpretation (S3). The eventual desensitization can be considered S1 therapist behavior. According to Lazarus, this case was treated successfully by using systematic desensitization. But the client was not desensitized regarding his fear of bridges. The desensitization focused on the client's mother's negative remarks about him, which may have resulted in a fear of responsibility. The fact that the first anxiety attack occurred while on a bridge may have linked the bridge with anxiety, thereby resulting in the phobic behavior.

It is clear that in any successful treatment process—and the emphasis here is on *successful*—therapist behaviors are diverse and match the client's readiness for the task at hand. The client in the foregoing example was willing and able to share his history with the therapist. A structured intake questionnaire (S1) that pertained to the phobic behavior would not only have been inappropriate but would no doubt have resulted in the client's being treated for the wrong problem.

Case Example: Hypnosis

The relationship between the ACT model and clinical hypnosis can be discussed on several levels. At one level, there is the issue of a client's readiness to be a hypnotic subject. Much of the hypnosis literature discusses who is a "good" subject—"good" subjects referring to those whose attitude and basic trust issues are such that they can be easily hypnotized. Assessing how good a potential hypnosis subject is can be likened to assessing how ready the client is within the ACT model. If the therapeutic task is to be hypnotized, then the client is highly ready if he or she is willing and able to be hypnotized.

At another level, induction techniques lend themselves to a comparison with ACT principles. Kohn (1984) describes induction techniques as classifiable on a continuum from authoritarian (direct) to permissive (indirect). It is interesting to note his instructions to the student therapist. In talking about how the student therapist might use induction techniques, he says (p. 23): "The beginning student can, if he wishes, employ them verbatim and later on modify and adapt them to his individual needs and style. However, the advanced student will find that as he gains experience, he will rely less on particular techniques or phraseology and more upon his own individual style and attitude. He may even find upon occasion he can obtain better results with no formal induction whatever.'' What a perfect statement that the more ready the student therapist, the less direction he or she will need for trance induction! The same point is made by Kohn regarding the subject. Authoritative techniques, if used at all by the clinical hypnotist, would be directed at those subjects who are most resistant to hypnosis. ''In the direct or authoritative technique, the subject is ordered, startled, or confused into hypnosis'' (Kohn, 1984, p. 25). Kohn, however, believes that trust and rapport are such critical elements in hypnotic work that clinical hypnotists are better off not using authoritative techniques at all. What is clear, as his discussion of induction continues, is that the subject new to the process of hypnosis (the less ready subject) requires more directiveness even in permissive techniques than the sophisticated subject (the more ready subject), who may only require a reminding word or two to fall into a trance.

A third level on which we can apply ACT to hypnosis is in examining the use of hypnosis as a treatment tool. ACT would describe hypnosis as a means for dealing with the client whose readiness level is characterized by ambivalent willingness. The client is trying to bring the problem to the surface, but his defenses stand in the way. Hypnosis becomes a method for going around these interfering defenses. Metaphorically it can be thought of as surgical anesthesia. It is difficult to perform surgery if the patient is awake. The patient's pain is an impediment to the surgeon's progress.

Clinical hypnosis is primarily an S2 treatment method. It is very supportive. The clinician is directive in terms of hypnotic suggestion, but the client is never ordered to move into a territory that is too threatening. By submitting to hypnosis, the client is, in one sense, willing to work on his ambivalent willingness. It is as if the client says to the therapist, ''I am willing to have you help me get to the root of the problem.'' The client's willingness can be seen in the following case:

Tom was a career man in the military, thirty-two years old, who came to me with the complaint that he had no feeling toward his ten-year-old son, and could not respond to him with affection whatever. In addition to his son, he had an eight-year-old daughter with whom he could relate in a normal affectionate manner.

For several sessions, he merely reiterated his complaint without being able to go into much detail. I was only able to obtain a very sketchy and vague history from him regarding past and present family relationships, and at the end of two or three sessions, I had little more information than I was able to obtain in the first ten minutes.

At that point, we decided to employ hypnosis. He readily entered a light to medium trance, as far as I was able to judge from his appearance and his report of his subjective reactions, although he was not able to respond with other typical hypnotic phenomena except a very slight ideomotor finger signal.

In subsequent sessions he had violent and emotional reactions and some rather dramatic insights. He saw his mother as unstable and unable to give him love, and as the result of some intense visual experiences in hypnosis, felt that his mother hated him because he loved his father. His father, he felt, was afraid to show him affection, just as the patient now is unable or afraid to show affection to his own son. It appeared that, at a subconscious level, he was not going to, or could not, give his son any affection since he received none from his father. Although this seemed to be one of the more important themes, there were other undercurrents such as the feeling that it was somehow shameful for a father to be demonstrative towards his son [Kohn, 1984, p. 84].

This case illustrates beautifully a client with ambivalent willingness. Without the use of hypnosis—without providing the direction and support of hypnotic suggestion—the important work of psychotherapy was at a standstill. The therapist began the treatment process with an S3 style because there was no reason to believe that the client's willingness and ability would require otherwise. Once the impasse was recognized, the therapist appropriately switched to an S2 position. The hypnosis is an effective treatment tool for putting the client at ease in order to allow his fears and conflicted feelings to surface.

Case Examples: Family Therapy

Family therapy frequently adopts a therapeutic stance that is both supportive and directive—an S2 stance. Most families come into treatment willing but unable. They want something to change; they want the problem to get better; they want to communicate; but they do not know how. They often need to be taught new ways of behaving and interacting with one another. The therapist becomes the teacher. This approach is illustrated in the following excerpt from a family therapy session (Grinder and Bandler, 1976, pp. 138–139):

Therapist:	Well, George (a ten-year-old boy), I've heard from all of the family members except you—tell me, what do you want?
George:	I want respect.
Matt:	(The father in the family) (Smiling broadly) Yes, that I believe.
George:	(Explosively) SEE!! That's just what I'm talking about—I don't get any respect from anyone in this family.
Therapist:	Wait, George; you sound real angry to me. Can you tell me what just happened with you?
George:	I . . . I . . . oh, never mind; you wouldn't understand anyway.

Therapist:	Perhaps not, but try me—did the way you just responded have something to do with something your father did?
George:	Yeah, I ask for respect and HE (pointing at his father, Matt) just laughs right out loud, making fun of me.
Matt:	That's not true. I didn't . . .
Therapist:	Be quiet for a moment, Matt. (Turning to George) George, tell exactly what happened with you just then.
George:	I asked for respect and my father started making fun of me—just the opposite.
Therapist:	George, tell me something—how, specifically, would you know that your father was respecting you?
George:	He wouldn't laugh at me—he would watch me when I say things and be serious about it.
Therapist:	George, I want to tell you something I noticed and something that I can see right now. Look at your father's face.
George:	Yeah, so what?
Therapist:	Well, does he look serious to you—does he look like he's taking you seriously right now—like he, maybe, respects you for what you're saying and doing right now?
George:	Yeah, you know he does look like he is.
Therapist:	Ask him, George.
George:	What . . . ask him . . . Dad do you respect me? Are you taking me seriously?
Matt:	Yes, son . . . (softly) . . . I'm taking you seriously right now. I respect what you're doing.
George:	(Crying softly) I really believe that you do, Dad.

> *Therapist:*   I have a hunch right now that Matt has
>   more to say, George; will you take him
>   (indicating Matt) seriously and listen
>   to him?
> *George:*   Sure . . .

With just a few minutes of teaching—of directing the
father and son in their interactions with one another—significant
progress is made. Two people who were unable to communicate
moments before become able to share a poignant moment
together. They wanted to be able to talk to one another, but
they did not know how. The therapist's S2 style encouraged
the process in the right direction. We can imagine the resulting
therapeutic fiasco if father and son were simply encouraged to
express all their feelings about one another with no direction
from the therapist. Or if the therapist, like George, began
demanding that the father behave differently. George and Matt's
readiness level made the *teaching* approach the treatment of
choice. They wanted to communicate with one another but did
not know how.

A slightly different course for treatment may be called for
if one or more family members in the therapy situation is severely
impaired. When this is the case, we might assume that the family
or certain family members are less willing or able than Matt
and George and will therefore require an even more directive
stance on the part of the therapist. Such was the case in a family
where one of the members, Gus, had been diagnosed as "borderline personality disorder, with possible temporal lobe seizures
in addition to some other seizure disorder. He said he was not
seriously suicidal, but I was worried about what he might do
impulsively" (Beels, 1977, p. 38). As ACT would predict, the
therapist in this situation needed to provide significant structure for this client. Consistent with the model, the therapist made
several beginning contracts with the members of this family,
among them an instruction to Gus that he was to see a neuro-
logist and a temporary mandate to Gus's wife that she was not
to threaten to leave Gus. ACT would agree that in this early
phase of the therapy process, specific contracts and specific in-

structions were necessary. As the family developed and became more ready in ACT terms, we assume that the therapist's behavior would change also. In fact, that is exactly what happened. Eight months later, with Gus on medication and family therapy in progress, Gus and his wife report that they feel great and think they have learned a lot.

In this chapter, we have examined a variety of cases from the literature to see if the ACT model holds up when applied to the casework of seasoned therapists. The cases we presented, like most of the cases described in the psychotherapy literature, had successful therapeutic outcomes. We were pleased, but not surprised, that our conception of a systematically eclectic approach to therapy held up so well in its applicability to the clinical work of a range of well-respected practitioners. For those of us who describe ourselves as eclectic, the range of potential treatment plans and therapist styles is impressive. ACT is a model that helps the clinician to narrow and focus the number of possible alternatives. By applying ACT to the broad range of cases in this chapter, we believe that we have demonstrated its applicability to a variety of client situations.

10

Adaptive Counseling and Therapy: Summary and Future Directions

ACT is built on the foundation of a rather simple belief: treatment and the behavior of the therapist should vary systematically according to the client's characteristics and the therapy's tasks or goals. The two dimensions on which the therapist's behavior vary are amount of direction and amount of support. The therapist's directive and supportive behavior comprise the therapist's style. This style is not a discrete measure but falls on a continuum. ACT divides that continuum into four quadrants labeled telling, teaching, supporting, and delegating. The *preferred* style is the style that a therapist is most comfortable using; style ranges refers to how many styles the therapist has at his or her command; style adaptability refers to how effective a therapist is at selecting the best-fitting therapy style.

The characteristics of the client that the therapist assesses in treatment planning are willingness (or motivation), ability (or competence), and confidence as these characteristics relate to the therapeutic task at hand. These three client characteristics comprise what ACT calls client task readiness. A client's readiness level depends on the task. Since many clients concurrently work on a variety of therapeutic tasks, we can assume that a client may be simultaneously exhibiting more than one readiness level.

As in other models of psychotherapy, ACT requires that the nature of the therapeutic problems be assessed, that the goals for treatment be determined, that a treatment plan be developed, and that therapeutic progress be monitored. ACT involves two levels of analysis in terms of treatment and treatment planning. The first level involves the specific treatment techniques and styles used by the therapist. The second level involves the form or the setting of treatment. Just as therapist style varies in directiveness and supportiveness according to the client's readiness level, so too does the form of treatment. Lastly, the better the match between the style of treatment and the client's readiness level, the more successful the outcomes of treatment are predicted to be. Successful therapy is a developmental process in which the client progresses from a less ready state to a more ready state in terms of accomplishing his or her designated therapeutic tasks.

Research and ACT

Since this is a book for practitioners, we have not dwelt on research issues related to ACT. While we have been empirically testing ACT in the clinical setting, however, there has been a concurrent effort to evaluate ACT in a more formalized manner. The TSI, which was presented in Chapter One, is offered as the cardinal measuring device of the therapist variables that are central to ACT theory. Two studies have been conducted to determine the sensitivity, reliability, and validity of the TSI (Gabbard and Howard, forthcoming; Gabbard, Howard, and Dunfee, 1986). A thorough review of these studies can be found in Howard, Nance and, Myers (1986).

Clinical Application of ACT

It is imperative, if ACT is to be a viable model, that its principles be applied to the practice of psychotherapy. ACT is not so much a theory about psychotherapy as it is a model to be used—a model with which the reader can experiment in clinical practice. ACT can be applied to the practice of counseling and therapy in a number of ways. For the eclectic practitioner, of course, adaptive counseling and therapy is a theoretical model for the practice of psychotherapy which, when applied to clinical casework, provides a systematic approach for selecting the best-fitting treatment plan and the most appropriate therapist styles for the client. ACT is an integrative tool that assists the practitioner in making good therapeutic decisions.

In discussing ACT, we have focused on presenting it primarily as a model for systematic eclecticism. Indeed we see this focus as ACT's major contribution. It is, however, a model that can be applied to the practice of psychotherapy in several other valuable ways. The therapist who specializes in a certain clinical approach can use ACT as a screening device for selecting appropriate clients. To use ACT for screening, one must clearly understand the relationship between one's therapeutic approach and the client's readiness level. If the assessment of client readiness is used initially for screening purposes, the clinician who decides to work with the client will continue to use the assessment for treatment planning.

ACT is also a clinical tool for practitioners who not only do individual psychotherapy but who often see more than one person at a time, such as marriage and family therapists or group therapists. In these instances, the therapist would be assessing the readiness level of the couple, the family or group, as well as the readiness of those who comprise the multiple client.

Moreover, the ACT model can be helpful when applied to case review. Even if ACT has not been consciously considered in treatment planning, it can serve as an evaluation device in the review process. Is the case progressing? If so, can progress be attributed to the fact that the client's readiness level and the therapist's approach are well matched? If the case has reached a stalemate, we believe that the application of ACT principles should help to activate progress.

Finally, ACT is obviously an important tool for training and supervision. Its very essence was culled from a leadership model—and teachers, trainers, and supervisors are leaders. We think you can see that just as one can provide therapy using any of the four styles, so too one can provide supervision with varying degrees of direction and support.

ACT as a Tool for Systematic Eclecticism

It is certainly our contention that the ACT model and its application to psychotherapy is both intriguing and professionally profitable. We hope others will find it so. Our own eclectic approaches to the practice of therapy and the rise of eclecticism in general suggest the continuing need for the development of integrative models. Raymond Corsini, in the acknowledgments to his book *Current Psychotherapies* (1984), summarized our belief that counseling and psychotherapy will profit from an integration of theoretical perspectives: ''It is my hope that *Current Psychotherapies* will serve a more important purpose than merely explaining some two dozen systems of psychotherapy. From the very beginning my aim has been to advance and improve psychotherapy. My view is that eventually a final psychotherapy will result from all the special uniting, in the same manner that small rivers unite to become the Mississippi.''

But we should be clear that we do not regard ACT as the only model that will unite all the special systems of psychotherapy into, as Corsini puts it, a final psychotherapy. We briefly reviewed a few integrative approaches to psychotherapy in Chapter One to suggest that ACT is *augmenting* the movement toward integrative, metatheoretical perspectives on counseling and psychotherapy. We consider ACT to be a helpful supplement to other integrative models—not a competitor. Our stance in this regard is based on our recognition that other integrative, metatheoretical approaches possess unique strengths that ACT does not possess. Arnold Lazarus (1986, p. 466) acknowledges ACT's unique contribution when he says:

> Howard, Nance, and Myers (1986) have taken us a few steps further than most by providing some elegant tactics for matching optimal leadership styles to particular clients at various stages of readiness. By drawing on Hersey and Blanchard's (1977) Situational Leadership Theory, the authors have added an important dimension to the strategic choice and determination of several critical client-

therapist interactions. As a strong advocate of "be-
spoke therapy," I am always thrilled to discover better ways of tapping into my clients' idiosyncracies,
so that the entire clinical cadence rests on custom-
made transactions, based on specifiable "check
points" and "markers," with minimal reliance
upon "intuition" and subjective judgment. In this
regard, the authors deserve praise for pointing the
way to some potentially significant pathways. But
an enlightened, eclectic psychotherapy will need far
more than this lone insight.

Lazarus's multimodal therapy can easily be considered
in tandem with ACT. For example, if a therapist determined
an S2 intervention as optimal, which among the thousands of
possible S2 interventions should the therapist choose? Enter
Lazarus's notion of modes of problem domains and related
concepts—matching interventions to problem modes, confronting problems through multiple modes of influence simultaneously, and so forth. Once selected, interventions will proceed in
an S2 manner. One can see how ACT and multimodal therapy
can act hand in glove to enrich the therapy assessment and treatment planning process.

In our opinion, ACT and the other integrative models
are compatible systems that should be used in conjunction with
one another. Our eclecticism is thorough! We advocate the adoption of multiple, integrative perspectives as the best approach
to Corsini's dream of a final psychotherapy.

References

Argyris, C. *Personality and Organization: The Conflict Between System and the Individual.* New York: Harper & Row, 1957.

Argyris, C. *Interpersonal Competence and Organizational Effectiveness.* Homewood, Ill.: Dorsey, 1962.

Argyris, C. *Integrating the Individual and the Organization.* New York: Wiley, 1964.

Arlow, J. A. "Psychoanalysis." In R. J. Corsini (ed.), *Current Psychotherapies.* (1st ed.) Itasca, Ill.: Peacock, 1977.

Bandler, R., and Grinder, J. *The Structure of Magic.* Palo Alto: Science and Behavior Books, 1975.

Bandura, A. "Self-Efficacy: Toward a Unifying Theory of Behavioral Change." *Psychological Review,* 1977, *84*, 191–215.

Beels, C. C. "The Identified Patient." In P. Papp (ed.), *Family Therapy: Full-Length Case Studies.* New York: Gardner Press, 1977.

Beutler, L. E. *Eclectic Psychotherapy: A Systematic Approach.* New York: Pergamon Press, 1983.

Blake, R. R., and Mouton, J. S. *The Managerial Grid.* Houston: Gulf Publishing, 1964.

Blanchard, K., and Johnson, S. *The One Minute Manager.* New York: William Morrow, 1982.

Blocher, D. H. *Developmental Counseling.* New York: Ronald Press, 1966.

Brammer, L. M., and Shostrom, E. L. *Therapeutic Psychology.* (3rd ed.) Englewood Cliffs, N.J.: Prentice-Hall, 1977.

Carkhuff, R. R., and Berenson, B. G. *Beyond Counseling and Therapy.* New York: Holt, Rinehart and Winston, 1967.

205

Cherniss, C., and Equatios, E. "Clinical Supervision in Community Mental Health." *Social Work,* 1977, *23,* 219–223.

Cohen, P. M. "Violence in the Family—an Act of Loyalty." *Psychotherapy,* 1984, *21* (2), 249–253.

Corsini, R. J. *Current Psychotherapies.* (3rd ed.) Itasca, Ill.: Peacock, 1984.

Ellis, A. *Reason and Emotion in Psychotherapy.* Secaucus, N.J.: Citadel Press, 1979.

Ellis, A., and Grieger, R. *Handbook of Rational-Emotive Therapy.* New York: Springer, 1977.

Ellis, A., and Harper, R. A. *A Guide to Rational Living.* Englewood Cliffs, N.J.: Prentice-Hall, 1961.

Fairbairn, W.R.D. *An Object-Relations Theory of Personality.* New York: Basic Books, 1952.

Fiedler, F. A. "A Comparison of Therapeutic Relationships in Psychoanalytic, Nondirective and Adlerian Therapy." *Journal of Consulting Psychology,* 1950, *14,* 436–445.

Fiedler, F. A. "Factor Analyses of Psychoanalytic, Nondirective, and Adlerian Therapeutic Relationships." *Journal of Consulting Psychology,* 1951, *15,* 32–38.

Frank, J. D. *Persuasion and Healing.* Baltimore: Johns Hopkins University Press, 1961.

French, J.R.P., and Raven, B. "The Bases of Social Power." In D. Cartwright (ed.), *Studies in Social Power.* Ann Arbor: University of Michigan Institute for Social Research, 1959.

Gabbard, C. E., and Howard, G. S. "Validity of the Adaptive Counseling and Therapy Model in Counselor Supervision." Manuscript submitted for publication (forthcoming).

Gabbard, C. E., Howard, G. S., and Dunfee, E. J. "Reliability, Sensitivity to Measuring Change, and Construct Validity of Therapist Adaptability." *Journal of Counseling Psychology,* 1986, *33,* 377–386.

Garfield, S. L. *Psychotherapy: An Eclectic Approach.* New York: Wiley, 1980.

Garfield, S. L., and Kurtz, R. A. "A Survey of Clinical Psychologists: Characteristics, Activities, and Orientations." *Clinical Psychologist,* 1974, *28,* 7–10.

Garfield, S. L., and Kurtz, R. A. "A Study of Eclectic Views." *Journal of Consulting and Clinical Psychology,* 1977, *45,* 78–83.

Getz, W., Wiesen, A. N., Sue, S., and Ayers, A. *Fundamentals of Crisis Counseling.* Lexington, Mass.: Lexington Books, 1974.

Glasser, W. *Reality Therapy.* New York: Harper & Row, 1965.

Glasser, W., and Zunin, L. M. "Reality Therapy." In R. J. Corsini (ed.), *Current Psychotherapies.* (2nd ed.) Itasca, Ill.: Peacock, 1979.

Goldfried, M. R. "Toward the Delineation of Therapeutic Change Principles." *American Psychologist,* 1980, *35*, 991–999.

Goldfried, M. R. (ed.). *Converging Themes in Psychotherapy: Trends in Psychodynamic, Humanistic, and Behavioral Practice.* New York: Springer, 1982.

Goldfried, M. R., and Padower, W. "Current Status and Future Directions in Psychotherapy." In M. R. Goldfried (ed.), *Converging Themes in Psychotherapy: Trends in Psychodynamic, Humanistic, and Behavioral Practice.* New York: Springer, 1982.

Gordon, C., and Beresin, E. "Conflicting Treatment Models: The Inpatient Management of Borderline Patients." *American Journal of Psychiatry,* 1983, *140* (8), 979–983.

Grinder, J., and Bandler, R. *The Structure of Magic II.* Palo Alto, Calif.: Science and Behavior Books, 1976.

Heller, K., Myers, R. A., and Kline, L. V. "Interviewer Behavior as a Function of Standardized Client Roles." *Journal of Counseling Psychology,* 1963, *27*, 117–122.

Hersey, P., and Blanchard, K. H. *Management of Organizational Behavior: Utilizing Human Resources.* (3rd ed.) Englewood Cliffs, N.J.: Prentice-Hall, 1977.

Highlin, P. S., and Hill, C. E. "Factors Affecting Client Change in Individual Counseling: Current Status and Theoretical Speculations." In S. D. Brown and R. W. Lent, *Handbook of Counseling Psychology.* New York: Wiley, 1984.

Howard, G. S., Nance, D. W., and Myers, P. "Adaptive Counseling and Therapy: An Integrative, Metatheoretical Approach." *Counseling Psychologist,* 1986, *14*, 363–442.

Hughes, J. D. "The Comparison of General and Specific Videotape Pretraining on Selected Process and Outcome Variables in Counseling." Unpublished doctoral dissertation, Indiana State University, 1983.

Ivey, A. E. "Counseling 2000: Time to Take Charge." *Counseling Psychologist,* 1980, *8* 12–16.

Kernberg, O. F. *Borderline Conditions and Pathological Narcissism.* New York: Jason Aronson, 1975.

Kohn, H. B. *Clinical Application of Hypnosis: A Manual for Health Professionals.* Springfield, Ill.: Thomas, 1984.

Korzybski, A. *Science and Sanity: An Introduction to Non-Aristotelian Systems and General Semantics.* Garden City, N.Y.: Country Life Press, 1950.

Kuhn, T. S. *The Structure of Scientific Revolutions.* (2nd ed.) Chicago: University of Chicago Press, 1970.

Lazarus, A. A. "In Support of Technical Eclecticism." *Psychological Reports,* 1967, *21*, 415–416.

Lazarus, A. A. *Behavior Therapy and Beyond.* New York: McGraw-Hill, 1971.

Lazarus, A. A. *Multimodal Behavior Therapy.* New York: Springer, 1976.

Lazarus, A. A. *The Practice of Multimodal Therapy.* New York: McGraw-Hill, 1981.

Lazarus, A. A. *Casebook of Multimodal Therapy.* New York: Guilford, 1985.

Lazarus, A. A. "Hard Sell for ACT Theory: Multimodal Therapy Shortchanged." *Counseling Psychologist,* 1986, *14*, 465–470.

Mahler, M. S. "A Study of the Separation-Individuation Process and Its Possible Application to Borderline Phenomena in the Psychoanalytic Situation." *Psychoanalysis,* 1971, *26*, 403–424.

Mandelbaum, A. "The Family Treatment of the Borderline Patient." In P. Hartocolles (ed.), *Borderline Personality Disorders: The Concept, the Syndrome, the Patient.* New York: International Universities Press, 1977.

Maslow, A. H. *Motivation and Personality.* New York: Harper & Row, 1954.

Meador, B. D., and Rogers, C. R. "Person-Centered Therapy." In R. J. Corsini (ed.), *Current Psychotherapies.* (2nd ed.) Itasca, Ill.: Peacock, 1979.

Meichenbaum, D. *Cognitive-Behavior Modification.* New York: Plenum Press, 1977.

Meichenbaum, D. H., and Goodman, J. "Training Impulsive Children to Talk to Themselves: A Means of Developing Self-Control." *Journal of Abnormal Psychology,* 1971, *77*, 115–126.

Minuchin, S. *Families and Family Therapy*. Cambridge, Mass.: Harvard University Press, 1974.

Mosak, H. H. "Adlerian Psychotherapy." In R. J. Corsini (ed.), *Current Psychotherapies*. (2nd ed.) Itasca, Ill.: Peacock, 1979.

Mosak, H. H., and Shulman, B. H. *Individual Psychotherapy: A Syllabus*. Chicago: Alfred Adler Institute, 1963.

Norcross, J. C. (ed.). *Handbook of Eclectic Therapy*. New York: Brunner/Mazel, 1986.

Parker, G. V. "Some Concomitants of Therapist Dominance in the Psychotherapy Interview." *Journal of Consulting Psychology*, 1967, *13*, 313–318.

Patterson, C. H. *Theories of Counseling and Psychotherapy*. (3rd ed.) New York: Harper & Row, 1980.

Paul, G. L. "Strategy of Outcome Research in Psychotherapy." *Journal of Consulting Psychology*, 1967, *39*, 109–118.

Perls, F. S. *Ego, Hunger and Aggression: The Beginning of Gestalt Therapy*. New York: Random House, 1969.

Prochaska, J. O. *Systems of Psychotherapy: A Transtheoretical Analysis*. Homewood, Ill.: Dorsey Press, 1979.

Rogers, C. R. *Counseling and Psychotherapy*. Cambridge, Mass.: Riverside Press, 1942.

Rogers C. R. *Client-Centered Therapy*. Boston: Houghton Mifflin, 1951.

Rogers, C. R. *On Becoming a Person*. Boston, Houghton Mifflin, 1961.

Skinner, B. F. *Beyond Freedom and Dignity*. New York: Knopf, 1971.

Smith, D. "Trends in Counseling and Psychotherapy." *American Psychologist*, 1982, *37*, 802–809.

Smith, M. L., Glass, G. V., and Miller, T. I. *The Benefits of Psychotherapy*. Baltimore: Johns Hopkins University Press, 1980.

Stogdill, R. M., and Coorn, A. E. *Leader Behavior: Its Description and Measurement*. Columbus: Bureau of Business Research, 1957.

Strong, S. R. "Counseling: An Interpersonal Influence Process." *Journal of Counseling Psychology*, 1968, *15*, 215–224.

Szasz, T. S. "Recollections of a Psychoanalytic Psychotherapy:

The Case of 'Prisoner K.'" In A. Burton (ed.), *Case Studies in Counseling and Psychotherapy*. Englewood Cliffs, N.J.: Prentice-Hall, 1959.

Tyler, L. E. "The Next Twenty Years." In J. M. Whiteley and B. R. Fretz (eds.), *The Present and Future of Counseling Psychology*. Monterey, Calif.: Brooks/Cole, 1980.

Wallace, E. R. *Dynamic Psychiatry in Theory and Practice*. Philadelphia: Lea & Febiger, 1983.

Index